IS THERE ANYTHING WRONG WITH
SEX BEFORE MARRIAGE?

Other booklets from *Searching Issues* include:

Why Does God Allow Suffering?
What About Other Religions?
How Does the New Age Movement Relate to Christianity?
What Is the Christian Attitude to Homosexuality?
Is There a Conflict Between Science and Christianity?
Is the Trinity Unbiblical, Unbelievable and Irrelevant?

Is There Anything Wrong with Sex Before Marriage?

NICKY GUMBEL

Alpha

First published by Kingsway Publications Ltd in 1994
as part of *Searching Issues*
First printed as a booklet 1999
Reprinted four times
New edition 2002
Reprinted 2004
This edition published by Alpha International in 2010

ISBN: 978 1 905887 56 9

Illustrations by Charlie Mackesy

Published by Alpha International
Holy Trinity Brompton
Brompton Road
London SW7 1JA
Email: publications@alpha.org

Contents

Is there Anything Wrong with Sex Before Marriage?

A major sexual revolution took place in the second half of the twentieth century. Our society became saturated with sexual stimulation in films, television, advertising and glossy magazines. It is not only the top shelf in newsagents which is devoted to sex; now the middle-shelf magazines tell you 'everything you wanted to know about sex, plus much much more'. Sex has become the idol of our times.

At the same time, another alarming revolution has taken place: marriage and family life is breaking down. A century ago the divorce rate was 200 per annum. By 1987 it had risen to 151,000 per annum – a three-fold increase since 1967 – and by 2002 the figure had reached 160,000 per annum. Almost one half of marriages now end in divorce. The financial cost of broken marriages, based on hard statistics such as legal aid and supplementary benefits, is a staggering £2 billion per year.[1] More importantly, the human cost is incalculable.

So we see in our society an increasing unwillingness to enter marriage in the first place. More and more couples live together without getting married. Only two in three conceptions now occur inside marriage and lead to birth. John Diamond wrote in *The Times*, 'Nowadays, for most people at least, marriage is one of those optional things you do if you want to make a particular sort of statement about the life you already share.'[2]

These changed attitudes to marriage and sex involve hidden dangers. Many people find themselves trapped in a promiscuity which destroys their self esteem, exposes them to sexually transmitted disease and often ruins their ability to form a lasting relationship. From the optimistic embrace of sexual liberation in the sixties, most people have started to see that there is something fundamentally wrong with this so called sexual liberation.

On the other hand, there have been times when the church and society have had a totally repressive and negative attitude towards sex. Origen, one of the early theologians of the church, regarded sex as something inherently sinful: 'Adam did not have sexual knowledge of his wife until after The Fall. If it had not been for The Fall, the human race would likely have been propagated in some very mysterious or angelic manner without sex and, therefore, sin.'

In the Middle Ages, Yves of Chartres taught that complete abstinence from sexual relationships had to be maintained on five out of seven days a week: on Thursdays in memory of the arrest of our Lord, on Fridays in honour of his death, on Saturdays in honour of the Virgin Mary, on Sundays in commemoration of the Resurrection, and on

Mondays out of respect for the faithful departed!

The Victorian era is also well-known for its sexual prudery when some even considered that the legs of pianos had to be covered! These prejudices and the sense of guilt associated with sex still affect the lives of many.

Both the obsession of the modern era and the repression of former times are a far cry from the biblical understanding of sex which is not outdated but highly relevant to us and our society today. Indeed, it is here that we find the Maker's instructions which bring liberation and fulfilment.

GOD, IN HIS LOVE, HAS GIVEN US A GOOD PLAN

The Bible affirms our sexuality: God made us 'male and female' (Genesis 1:27). The body is good; we are 'fearfully and wonderfully made' (Psalm 139:14). Jesus had a physical body. Everything God made was good – including our sexual organs which he designed for our enjoyment. The sexual urge is God-given and, like fire in the fireplace, is a great blessing when enjoyed in the right context. In God's original creation Adam and Eve were 'both naked, and they felt no shame' (Genesis 2:25). There was no guilt attached to their sexuality, which is why we should be able to talk openly and frankly about these matters without embarrassment. As C. S. Lewis points out, 'Pleasure is God's idea, not the Devil's.' God is not looking down from heaven and saying, 'Goodness gracious, whatever will they get up to next?'

Further, the Bible celebrates sexual intimacy as a profound form of communication. 'Adam knew Eve his wife, and she conceived and bore Cain' (Genesis 4:1, RSV). In the Song of Solomon we see the delight, tenderness, contentment and satisfaction that can be derived from sexual intimacy. The tone is set in the opening verses: 'Let him kiss me with the kisses of his mouth – for your love is more delightful than wine' (Song of Songs 1:2).

Sex in its right context is good and beautiful. God has a high view of sexual relationships. Marriage is a reflection of Christ's relationship with the church (Ephesians 5) and there can be nothing higher than that. That is why Christian married couples should be encouraged to delight in one another and enjoy sexual intimacy to the full. There is great freedom within marriage and sex should never become mundane or boring. This contrasts sharply with the attitude of many so-called defenders of sexual liberation. Marcelle d'Argy Smith, editor of *Cosmopolitan*, said recently, 'Sex is like Big Ben. I'm glad it's there and if I were less tired I could go and have a look at it.'[3]

The biblical context of sexual intercourse is the lifelong commitment in marriage between one man and one woman. When Jesus spoke of marriage he went back to the creation account: 'For this reason a man will leave his father and mother and be united to his wife, and they will become one flesh' (Matthew 19:5–6 quoting Genesis 2:24).

Here we see the key to the biblical understanding of marriage. First, there is a leaving – a public act of lifelong exclusive commitment. Secondly, there is a uniting of the man and the woman. They are 'glued together' in marriage. Thirdly, it is in this context that the 'one flesh' sexual union takes place. It is not just physical and biological, but emotional, psychological, spiritual and social. Our whole beings are united in marriage, and sexual intercourse is not just a physical response to a physical desire. The physical union both expresses the other unions and also brings them about. We express ourselves with our bodies and the act of intercourse expresses our unity. 'The total physical self-giving would be a lie if it were not the sign and fruit of a total personal self-giving . . . The only "place" in which this self-giving in its whole truth is made possible is marriage.'[4]

God has so designed our bodies and our sexuality that we can go on exploring and enjoying one another for a lifetime. An actor, well-known for his romantic roles, was asked on a TV programme, 'What makes a great lover?' He answered: 'A great lover is someone who can satisfy one woman all her life long; and who can be satisfied by one woman all his life long. A great lover is not someone who goes from woman to woman. Any dog could do that.' Of course, this applies to men and women alike.

Next, in God's order, partnership and procreation are linked. God blessed Adam and Eve and said to them, 'Be fruitful and increase in number' (Genesis 1:28). God so designed our bodies that the same act of intercourse should have the effect of both uniting us in partnership and being the means by which procreation takes place. This does not mean that every act of intercourse should have that intention, but it is part of God's design that it takes a man and a woman to have a baby. God's ideal is that every child should be conceived in an act that expresses love and commitment and that they should grow up in that atmosphere. The most important relationship for a child's security is the one between the two parents.

GOD, IN HIS LOVE, WARNS AGAINST HUMAN DISTORTIONS

Tragically, God's plan has been distorted by human sin. Our sin affects every area of our human lives, including our sexuality. 'All have sinned and fall short of the glory of God'

(Romans 3:23). Obviously, not everyone's sexuality is equally distorted, and some will retain the original creation order more than others, but none of us is in a position to pass judgement. When Jesus said to those about to stone the woman caught in adultery: 'Let anyone of you who is without sin be the first to throw a stone at her' (John 8:7), the context was not just any sin, but specifically sexual sin.

The fact that we are all guilty does not mean that it does not matter, or that we should make no attempt to avoid sin. Jesus told the woman, 'Leave your life of sin' (John 8:11). The Maker's instructions were given out of love. It is not that when he sees people enjoying themselves he says, 'I'll soon put a stop to that!' but rather that God does not want us to get hurt.

As we have seen, God designed sexual intercourse for our enjoyment in the context of marriage. Any sex outside marriage is a distortion of God's good gift and falls short of his ideal. Jesus took the Bible as his authority and if Jesus is our Lord we must follow his example. This does not mean we condemn the people involved, for we are called to accept and love people unconditionally. At the same time, we must speak out against the sin. Indeed, it is part of loving people.

Any sex outside marriage is forbidden. Adultery is specifically outlawed by the seventh commandment, and when we see the betrayal of trust and the wreckage of families stemming from this deceit we are able to understand why. However, sex before marriage is certainly widely defended and needs more discussion.

Because sexual intercourse is a life-uniting act, Paul says that even if a man has sex with a prostitute he becomes 'one with her in body' (1 Corinthians 6:16). He commands his readers to 'flee from sexual immorality' (v.18). The word he uses includes all sex outside marriage. It is the same word that Jesus used in Mark 7: 21 and Paul used elsewhere (1 Thessalonians 4:3–8).

Most would agree that sex and love should go together. Promiscuity, although common practice today, has few serious defenders, but many people would defend the practice of sex before marriage in a more stable relationship. The teaching of Jesus in the rest of the New Testament is against such a practice, for it is not just love and sex that must go together but sex and long-term commitment to each other in marriage. Such commitment is evidenced in our society by the marriage vows. Marriage is not just a piece of paper, nor is the wedding day simply for dressing-up and getting together with family and friends. It is a public and responsible expression of lifelong commitment, and the certificate of marriage is a public document accessible to all. In this context, sexual intercourse signifies, seals and brings about an unbreakable, total personal unity. Without such a commitment, sex is cheapened, being 'a life-uniting act without a life-uniting intent'.[5] The life-uniting intent is evidenced by marriage alone; engagement is not sufficient, for engagements can always be broken (this is part of the point of a period of engagement). Irrevocable commitment comes only with the public act of marriage.

This is God's pattern for sexual relationships. Sex outside marriage may feel good. However, when God's pattern is broken people get hurt.

First, we risk hurting ourselves. When a relationship

14

involving sexual intercourse breaks down, one or both parties get hurt. This is true both in the case of divorce and in sexual relationships between unmarried people. Pre-marital sex increases the chances of extra-marital sex and, of course, adultery is one of the leading factors in marriage breakdown. Marriage is far more likely to work if the couple have not lived together. Recent figures have indicated that the divorce rate is far lower among those who have waited until their wedding day. For example, according to recent research of couples who married for the first time in the 1980s, those who lived together before marriage were 60 per cent more likely to have divorced after eight years of marriage than similar couples who had not done so.[6]

If we keep to God's laws, we live under his blessing, and part of that blessing will be the blessing of the wedding day. Even those who are not Christians often recognise that they have lost something by living together before the marriage. John Diamond, writing in *The Times* about those who have waited until their wedding day, says they

> have something to look forward to. They leave their parents' home on the morning of the wedding as children and climb into bed that night as adults. There is so much to play with, and all at the same time: the new house, the giggling joint washing-up sessions, the bed, the joint cheque book – and because it all started with the wedding, it all becomes part of the same adventure.
>
> The rest of us, the over-the-broomstick lot, get up, tap our partners on the shoulder, make jokey gulping noises, get a mini-cab round to the register office, listen to our mates making faux-ironic jokes about what we will be getting up to

tonight, ho-ho, and then come back and do last night's washing-up. We try out the new Mr and Mrs names for a day or two, then realise that our joint cheque book and the mortgage deeds are in the old names anyway, and go back to them.

We've done cheque books a dozen times and deciding on the new paint for the hall a hundred. There is nothing new you can tell us about the socks-on-the-bathroom-floor conundrum; and whose-turn-is-it-for-Waitrose mantra is one that we already know by heart. While newly met newlyweds can set sail on their magical voyage of discovery, our own marital plans mean we are stuck on the Woolwich ferry arguing about who forgot to bring the packed lunch.[7]

If two people who are already involved in a sexual relationship do eventually marry each other, they often regret that they did not wait until their wedding day.

The Revd Gordon Harman recalls from his childhood that he and his brother once came across an old black trunk whilst playing in a storeroom at their home. When they took the lid off, they discovered to their delight a complete model railway. They loved it, and felt sure it would be theirs one day. As each Christmas came and went, they experienced first disappointment and then guilt. Finally, the real day came and they put on a pretence of surprise, but both knew that they had partly ruined the gift.

When we embark on a sexual relationship at the wrong time we often induce patterns of guilt and frustration and run the risk of tainting the gift of our sexuality. People often say that they have sensed an indefinable purity and beauty at a wedding where both the husband and wife have waited for

16

each other. One couple I know who did sleep together before marriage say that one of their greatest regrets is not to have experienced that God-given blessing on their own wedding day.

Secondly, we risk hurting others. If a sexual relationship does not last, it may have a damaging effect on a future marriage. Previous sexual relationships can lead to jealousy and resentment for the uniqueness of the sexual act has been compromised. It can be particularly difficult when a husband or wife comes into contact with a previous partner.

Sexual relationships before marriage can make marriage itself less likely. Although our society apparently accepts the idea of a string of sexual relationships, there are not many people who set out to marry someone with a long and complex sexual past. The hurt involved can be very serious. If there is an unwanted pregnancy, then hard decisions have to be made.

Thirdly, we risk hurting society. The family unit is one of the basic building blocks of society. Increasingly, it is recognised that sex outside marriage can be a factor that leads to family breakdown. In turn, family breakdown is one of the reasons for the soaring crime rate. In fact, both are symptoms of a society which has turned away from God's standards. Immanuel Jakobovits, Chief Rabbi from 1967–1991, writing about marital infidelity, said that 'the cost to society is incalculable: above all in terms of the millions of children now being raised in a moral wasteland, without the shelter of a loving home. Is it any wonder that from their number countless embittered, selfish, lonely and sometimes violent citizens are recruited to swell the ranks of the anti-social?'[8]

Before AIDS promiscuity was unhealthy; now it can be fatal. For too long the glossy magazines fooled us that 'free love' was free. But there is a price to be paid. If we had kept to God's standards, AIDS would not have spread. The best way to stop it now is to return to God's standards.

Fourthly, we hurt God. The most important consideration of all is that breaking God's laws has serious consequences: it cuts us off from him. That is why it is impossible to hold together a wholehearted love and service of God and disobedience in the area of sexual morality. It is this which stops many today giving their lives to Christ, and they lose out on abundant and eternal life for something which in the long run only does them harm. Others are torn apart by the tension in their lives between a supposed profession of faith and a life which they know goes against such a profession.

The New Testament warns us that God will judge all sin, including immorality (1 Thessalonians 4:6). God's laws are there to protect us and to protect society – given out of love. But there are serious consequences when we break his laws.

GOD, IN HIS LOVE, SENT JESUS TO RESTORE US

God's standards are very high and in our society they are not easy to keep. However, God has not left us alone and he came to set us free. He did not come to condemn the world but to save it, giving us the power to resist temptation, and to bring forgiveness and healing.

How to resist
It is possible to stop having sexual intercourse, even though

it may be very difficult. When someone comes to Christ, they may be in a sexual relationship with a partner who is not a Christian. It may be hard to explain to that person why they will not have sex with them any more, and it could result in feelings of rejection and hurt. Yet it is almost impossible to make any real progress in the Christian faith until such a sexual relationship ends, because we cannot hold on to sin and be wholehearted in our Christian lives at the same time. If both parties come to Christ at the same time, it is easier, but it still requires great self-control. I have seen several couples who have succeeded in this area and have found enrichment from God in their relationship. Usually they have married later and found God's blessing also in their family life. Some think they will lose the respect of their friends, but the opposite is often the case. If we live by these standards we will have an opportunity to influence society, rather than being squeezed into the world's mould.

Many fear that there will be a gap in their lives if they stop making love, and that they will not be as close to their partner. This is not the case unless sex is the sole basis for the relationship, in which case it is better that the relationship ends because it lacks a solid foundation. Indeed, this is one of the dangers of sex before marriage: it clouds our judgement about the rightness of the relationship. It is much easier to work out whether we are suited to be partners for life if our judgement is unclouded by a sexual relationship. As one twenty-seven-year-old woman put it: 'Once the sex had been taken away, I realised there was nothing left.' If the relationship is right, there will not be such a gap; rather there will be a depth of understanding, respect, trust and dignity.

There may even be a sense of relief. Another woman said, 'I felt as though a huge weight, which I hadn't realised was there, lifted off my shoulders.' Sexual intercourse is not the only way to demonstrate love. In fact, self-control often shows more love and sets a good pattern for married life when, from time to time, self-control needs to be exercised. If the relationship is conducted along these lines it makes it easier for both parties to decide whether or not it is right to get married.

How do we avoid getting into such a situation in the first place? Jesus began with the heart, the eyes and the thoughts. He said, 'Anyone who looks at a woman lustfully has already committed adultery with her in his heart' (Matthew 5:28). This is where self-control begins for us all. All of us will be tempted to have immoral thoughts – Jesus was tempted also – but temptation is not sin. It is not the thoughts that are sinful; rather it is the entertaining of them. The more we give in, the more difficult it gets. The more we resist, the easier it gets. James, the brother of Jesus, wrote, 'Resist the devil, and he will flee from you. Come near to God and he will come near to you' (James 4:7–8). It tends to be a spiral, either going up or down.

We need to help one another by not putting temptation in the way. For example, it is not a good idea to sleep in the same bed if you are trying to resist temptation. Single people sometimes ask, 'How far can we go?' The Bible does not lay down the rules and nor should we. People and circumstances vary. We need to remember that it is always hard not to go further next time. It is also worth considering how you would feel if the relationship did end. It is much easier to maintain respect, dignity and friendship if you have exercised restraint in this area.

If the relationship continues to marriage, nothing is lost. In fact, the reverse is true. No married couple I know ever regretted going too slowly before they were married.

If all this leads then to great sexual frustration, is masturbation a way out? This can be a taboo subject, especially among Christian people. In fact, nearly all adolescents and many adults do masturbate. It is estimated that 95 per cent of men and over 50 per cent of women have some experience of masturbation. Of course, it is not physically harmful and it is nowhere specifically condemned in the Bible.

However, there are three concerns. First, it has a tendency to become obsessive. Secondly, it depersonalises sex – our sexuality was intended to move us towards personal communion. Thirdly, it is often associated with lustful thoughts. But the guilt that usually accompanies masturbation is out of all proportion to its seriousness. Martin Luther describes it as 'a puppy sin'. One pastor said it was like 'biting our nails' – something many do as part of growing up. It is not a good idea, but should not be taken too seriously unless it becomes excessive.

In all these areas we need to avoid the guilt and condemnation spiral which can bring us down and lead us to further sin. The Spirit of God sets us free where a set of rules would be powerless (Romans 8:1–4). Jesus' provision of the Holy Spirit means that it is possible to break free.

Forgiveness

As we have seen earlier, all of us have failed in this area to a greater or lesser extent. None of us is in a position to throw stones at anyone else. Jesus died for us so that we could be forgiven. The way to receive forgiveness is through repentance. In Psalm 51 we see a model for repentance following sexual sin. This is the psalm attributed to David after he had committed adultery with Bathsheba. The remedy for sin is not to make excuses or to do things to make up for it. Rather it is confession and repentance. However far we have fallen, we can make a new start in Christ.

I love the story Jackie Pullinger tells of a seventy-two-year-old woman in her church who was a heroin addict and a prostitute for sixty years. She used to sit outside a brothel waiting for customers, poking the sewers with a stick so that they would flow more freely. She was being injected in her back three times a day because there were no more veins in her arms and legs. She had no identity card and did not even exist as far as the Hong Kong government was concerned. She was 'one of those who are not'. Seven years ago she gave her life to Jesus Christ and received forgiveness for her sins. She went to live in one of Jackie's houses and God started to heal her. In the summer of 1992, she married Little Wa who was aged seventy-five. Jackie described it as 'the wedding of the decade'. The former prostitute was able to walk down the aisle in white, cleansed and forgiven by Jesus Christ.

Jesus enables us both to receive forgiveness and to give it. Many have been sinned against in this area. Some say that one person in ten has been sexually abused, and often people go through life crippled by these experiences. Freedom always begins with forgiveness – receiving God's forgiveness and then, in gratitude for his forgiveness, forgiving those who have sinned against us.

CONCLUSION

The heart of our sexuality is not the biological dimension but the personal one. Jesus himself points the way to a state beyond marriage. In heaven there will be no marriage. Here on this earth, as John Stott, himself unmarried, writes,

> it is possible for human sexual energy to be redirected ('sublimated' would be the Freudian word) both into affectionate relationships with friends of both sexes and into the loving service of others. Multitudes of Christian singles, both men and women, can testify to this. Alongside a natural loneliness, accompanied sometimes by acute pain, we can find joyful self-fulfilment in the self-giving service of God and other people.[9]

Sex is not an ultimate goal. Our society, as we have seen at the beginning, has made an idol out of sex. Sex has replaced God as the object of worship. We need to reverse this. If we seek pleasure as a god, in the long run we find emptiness, disappointment and addiction. If we seek God, we find, among other things, ecstatic pleasure.

FOR FURTHER READING

Lewis Smedes, *Sex for Christians* (Triangle SPCK, 1993).
Richard Foster, *Money, Sex and Power* (Hodder & Stoughton, 1985).
John White, *Eros Defiled* (IVP, 1977).

NOTES

1.   Statistics from *The Times* (31st May 1989).
2.   *The Times* (21st May 1992).
3.   *Daily Mail* (9th February 1993).
4.   Pope John Paul II, *Familiaris Consortio: Theology of the Body* (The Vatican, 1981), p11.
5.   Lewis Smedes, *Sex for Christians* (Triangle, SPCK, 1993), p130.
6.   John Haskey. Pre-marital cohabitation and the probability of divorce: analyses using new data from the General Household Survey. *Population Trends 68* (HMSO Publications), quoted in *The Times* (19th June 1992).
7.   *The Times* (25th June 1992).
8.   *The Times* (22nd September 1993).
9.   John Stott, *The Message of the Thessalonians* (IVP, 1991), pp84–85.

The Alpha Course

The Alpha course is a practical introduction to the Christian faith initiated by Holy Trinity Brompton in London, and now being run by thousands of churches, of many denominations, throughout the world.

For more information about Alpha, and related ministries such as The Marriage Course and The Marriage Preparation Course, please visit:

alpha.org

Or contact:
Alpha International
Holy Trinity Brompton
Brompton Road, London, SW7 1JA
0845 644 7544
info@alpha.org

If you would like a copy of the Alpha Publications Brochure, outlining details of resources available for purchase, or to order course materials, please contact the Alpha Publications Hotline on:

Tel: 0845 7581 278
Or visit: **alphashop.org**
To order from overseas:
Tel: +44 1228 611749

Alpha

Alpha titles available

Why Jesus? A booklet given to all participants at the start of the Alpha course. 'The clearest, best illustrated and most challenging short presentation of Jesus that I know.' – Michael Green

Why Christmas? The Christmas version of *Why Jesus?*

Questions of Life The Alpha course in book form. In fifteen compelling chapters Nicky Gumbel points the way to an authentic Christianity which is exciting and relevant to today's world.

A Life Worth Living What happens after Alpha? Based on the book of Philippians, this is an invaluable next step for those who have just completed the Alpha course, and for anyone eager to put their faith on a firm biblical footing.

How to Run the Alpha Course: Telling Others The theological principles and the practical details of how courses are run. Each alternate chapter consists of a testimony of someone whose life has been changed by God through an Alpha course.

The Jesus Lifestyle (formerly, *Challenging Lifestyle*) Studies in the Sermon on the Mount showing how Jesus' teaching flies in the face of modern lifestyle and presents us with a radical alternative.

30 Days Nicky Gumbel selects thirty passages from the Old and New Testament which can be read over thirty days. It is designed for those on an Alpha course and others who are interested in beginning to explore the Bible.

The Heart of Revival Ten Bible studies based on the book of Isaiah, drawing out important truths for today by interpreting some of the teaching of the Old Testament prophet Isaiah. The book seeks to understand what revival might mean and how we can prepare to be part of it.

All titles are by Nicky Gumbel, who is Vicar of Holy Trinity Brompton

The Ukulele playlist

Shows

C000076087

© 2013 by Faber Music Ltd
First published in 2013 by Faber Music Ltd
Bloomsbury House
74–77 Great Russell Street
London WC1B 3DA

Arranged by Alex Davis
Edited by Lucy Holliday

Designed by Sue Clarke
Photography by Ben Turner

Printed in England by Caligraving Ltd
All rights reserved

ISBN10: 0-571-53773-1
EAN13: 978-0-571-53773-0

buy Faber Music publications or to find out about
the full range of titles available, please contact your
ocal music retailer or Faber Music sales enquiries:

Faber Music Ltd, Burnt Mill, Elizabeth Way,
Harlow, CM20 2HX England

Tel: +44(0)1279 82 89 82
Fax: +44(0)1279 82 89 83

sales@fabermusic.com
fabermusicstore.com

Tuning

The standard Ukulele string tuning is G–C–E–A, shown here on the treble stave and piano keyboard. Note that the G string is tuned higher than the C string.

You can tune your Ukulele using a piano or keyboard (or any other instrument that you know is in tune!) or by using an electronic chromatic tuner.

If just one string on your Ukulele is in tune then you can use it to tune the other strings as well.

This diagram shows which fretted notes match the note of the open string above. Eg. Pluck the first string at the 5th fret and match the note to the second open string, and so on.

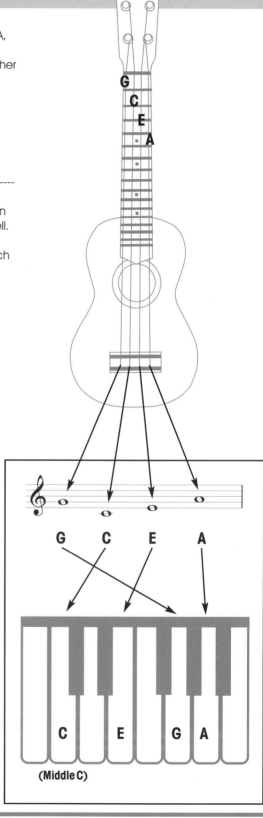

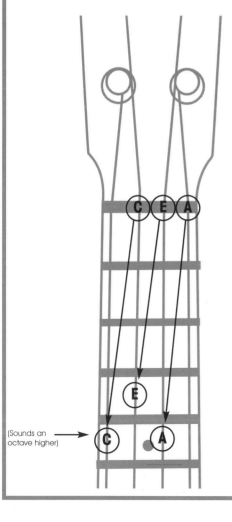

(Sounds an octave higher)

(Middle C)

And All That Jazz

Words by Fred Ebb
Music by John Kander

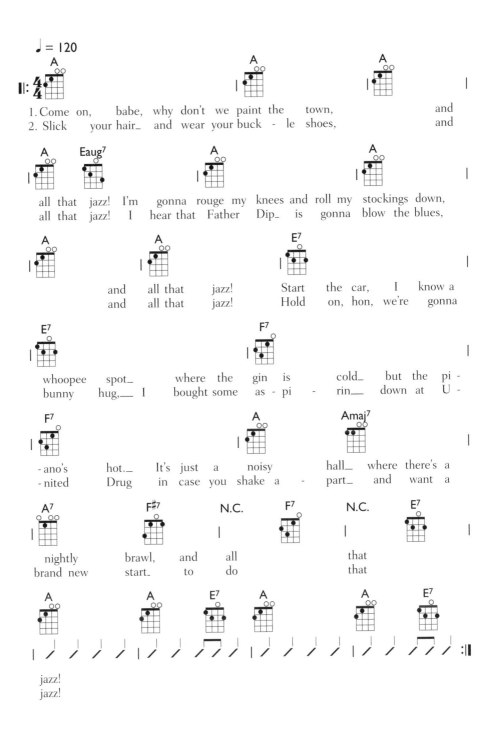

4

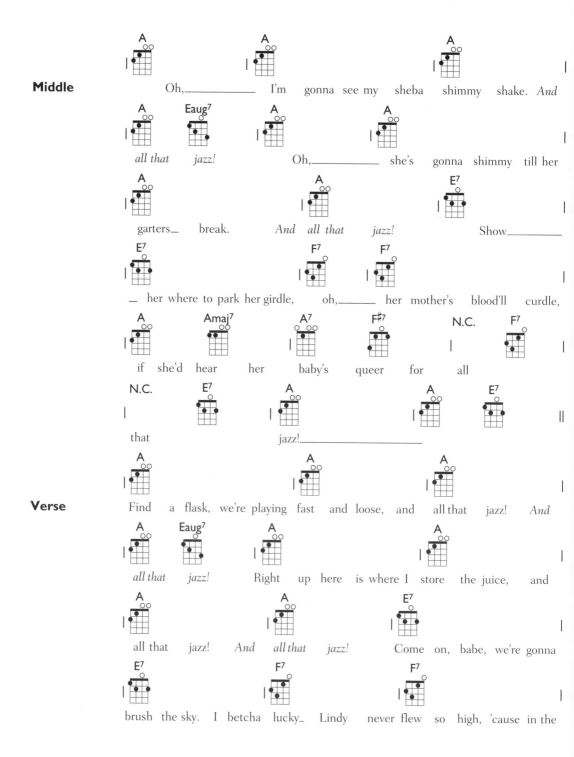

Middle
Oh,_____ I'm gonna see my sheba shimmy shake. *And*

all that jazz! Oh,_____ she's gonna shimmy till her

garters_ break. *And all that jazz!* Show_____

_ her where to park her girdle, oh,_____ her mother's blood'll curdle,

if she'd hear her baby's queer for all

that jazz!_____

Verse
Find a flask, we're playing fast and loose, and all that jazz! *And*

all that jazz! Right up here is where I store the juice, and

all that jazz! *And all that jazz!* Come on, babe, we're gonna

brush the sky. I betcha lucky_ Lindy never flew so high, 'cause in the

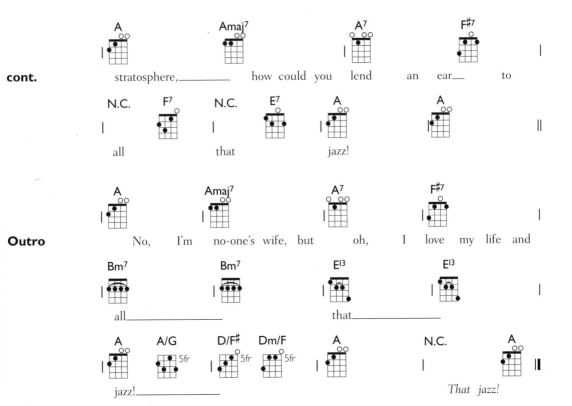

cont.

A	Amaj⁷	A⁷	F♯⁷
stratosphere,_____	how could you	lend an ear__	to

N.C. F⁷	N.C. E⁷	A	A
all	that	jazz!	

Outro

A	Amaj⁷	A⁷	F♯⁷
No, I'm	no-one's wife, but	oh, I	love my life and

Bm⁷	Bm⁷	E¹³	E¹³
all_____		that_____	

A A/G D/F♯ Dm/F	A	N.C. A
jazz!_____		*That jazz!*

6

Any Dream Will Do

Lyrics by Tim Rice
Music by Andrew Lloyd Webber

♩ = 125

Verses

C | G
1. I closed my eyes,___ drew back the
2. May I re - turn. *May I re - turn.* To the be -

C | F | C
curtain___ to see for certain___
- ginning,_ *(Aah)*___ the light is dimming,___ *(Aah)*___

G | C | G
what I thought I knew.___ Far far a -
___ and the dream is too.___ The world and

C | G | C | F
- way,___ someone was weeping,___ but the world was
I, *(The world and I)* we are still waiting, *(Aah)*_ still he - si -

C | G | C | G
sleeping,___ any dream will do.___ I wore my
- ta - ting, *(Aah)*_ any dream will do.___ *Instrumental*

C | G | C | F
coat, *(I wore my coat)* with golden lining,_ *(Aah)*_ bright colours

C | G | C | G
shining_ *(Aah)*_ wonderful and new.___ And in the

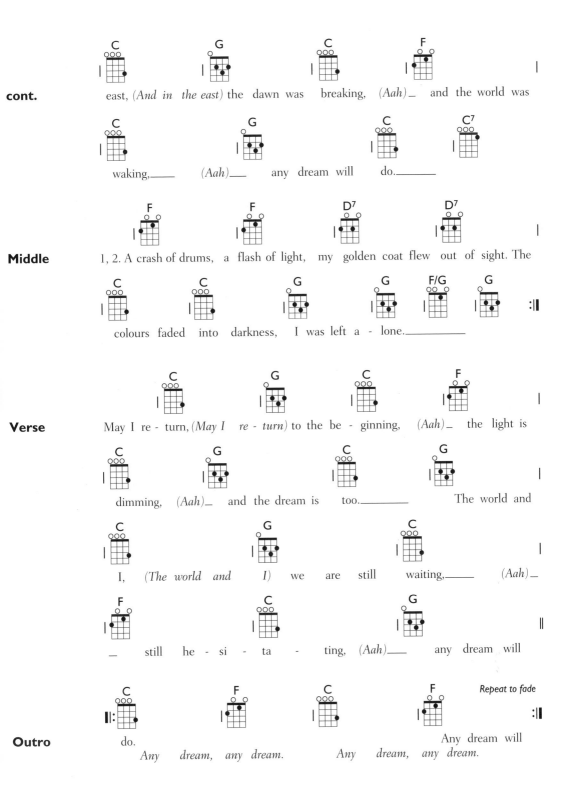

cont. east, *(And in the east)* the dawn was breaking, *(Aah)* and the world was

waking, *(Aah)* any dream will do.

Middle 1, 2. A crash of drums, a flash of light, my golden coat flew out of sight. The

colours faded into darkness, I was left a - lone.

Verse May I re - turn, *(May I re - turn)* to the be - ginning, *(Aah)* the light is

dimming, *(Aah)* and the dream is too. The world and

I, *(The world and I)* we are still waiting, *(Aah)*

still he - si - ta - ting, *(Aah)* any dream will

Repeat to fade

Outro do. Any dream will

Any dream, any dream. *Any dream, any dream.*

Cabaret

Words by Fred Ebb
Music by John Kander

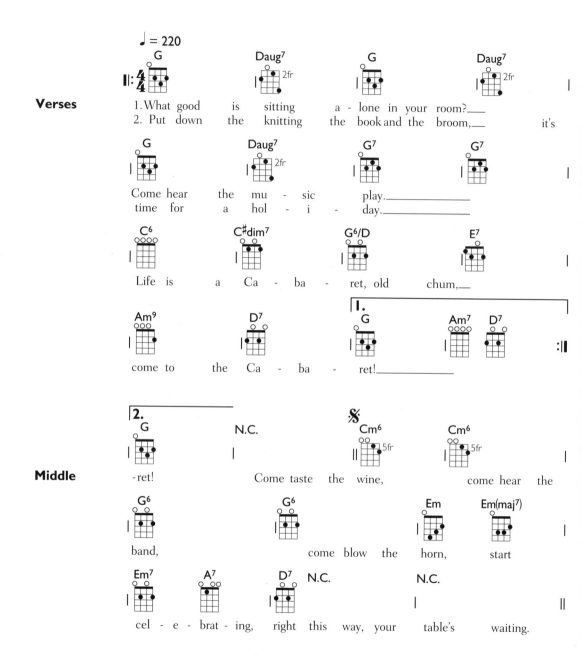

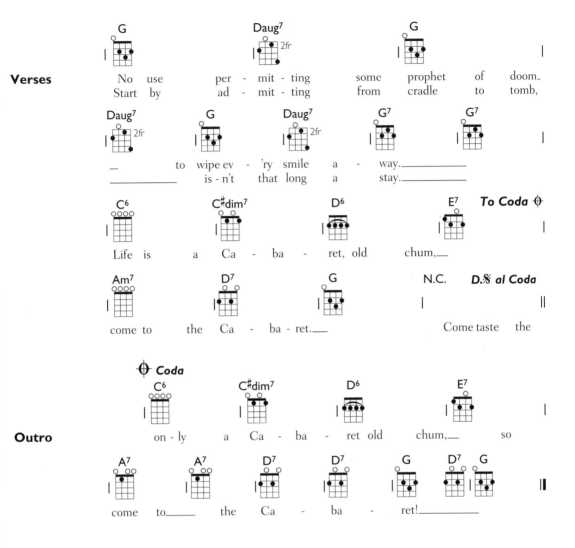

Verses

G — No use / Start by
Daug7 — per - mit - ting / ad - mit - ting
G — some prophet / from
prophet of doom / cradle to
doom_ / tomb,

Daug7 — _ / _____
G — to wipe ev / is - n't
Daug7 — 'ry smile / that long
G7 — a - way._____ / a stay._____
G7 — a / a

C6 — Life is
C#dim7 — a Ca - ba -
D6 — ret, old
E7 — chum,__   **To Coda** ⊕

Am7 — come to
D7 — the Ca - ba - ret.__
G —
N.C. — Come taste the   **D.% al Coda**

⊕ **Coda**

Outro

C6 — on - ly
C#dim7 — a Ca - ba -
D6 — ret old
E7 — chum,__ so

A7 — come
A7 — to___
D7 — the Ca -
D7 — ba -
G — ret!_____
D7 G

Can You Feel The Love Tonight

Words by Tim Rice
Music by Elton John

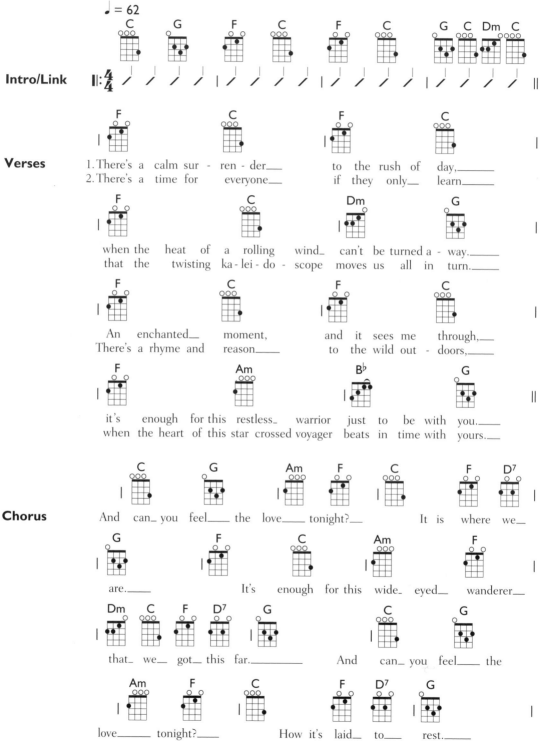

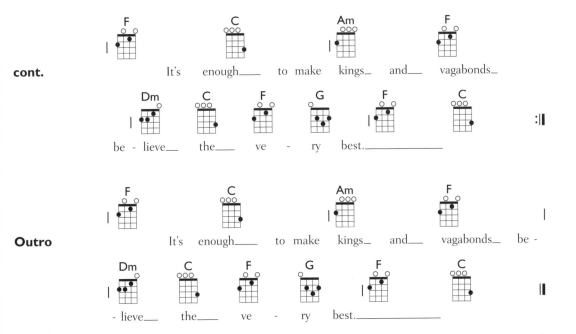

cont.
F   C   Am   F

It's   enough___   to make   kings_   and__   vagabonds_

Dm   C   F   G   F   C

be - lieve__   the__   ve - ry   best._____

Outro
F   C   Am   F

It's   enough___   to make   kings_   and__   vagabonds_   be -

Dm   C   F   G   F   C

- lieve__   the__   ve - ry   best._____

Consider Yourself

Words and Music by Lionel Bart

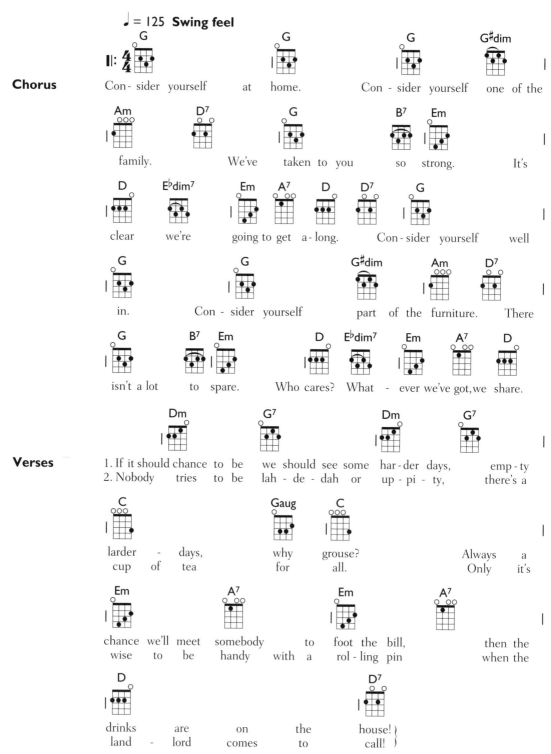

♩ = 125 **Swing feel**

Chorus

Con- sider yourself   at   home.   Con - sider yourself   one of the

family.   We've   taken to you   so   strong.   It's

clear   we're   going to get a- long.   Con - sider yourself   well

in.   Con - sider yourself   part   of the furniture.   There

isn't a lot   to   spare.   Who cares?   What - ever we've got, we   share.

Verses

1. If it should chance to be   we should see some har-der days,   emp-ty
2. Nobody   tries   to be   lah - de - dah   or   up-pi - ty,   there's a

larder   - days,   why   grouse?   Always   a
cup   of   tea   for   all.   Only   it's

chance we'll meet   somebody   to   foot the bill,   then the
wise   to   be   handy   with   a   rol - ling pin   when the

drinks   are   on   the   house!)
land   - lord   comes   to   call!)

13

Chorus

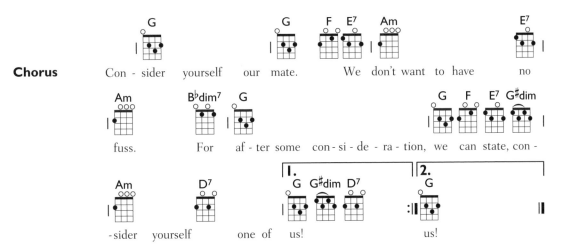

Con - sider yourself our mate. We don't want to have no

fuss. For af - ter some con - si - de - ra - tion, we can state, con -

-sider yourself one of us! us!

Don't Leave Me This Way

Words and Music by Kenneth Gamble, Leon Huff and Cary Gilbert

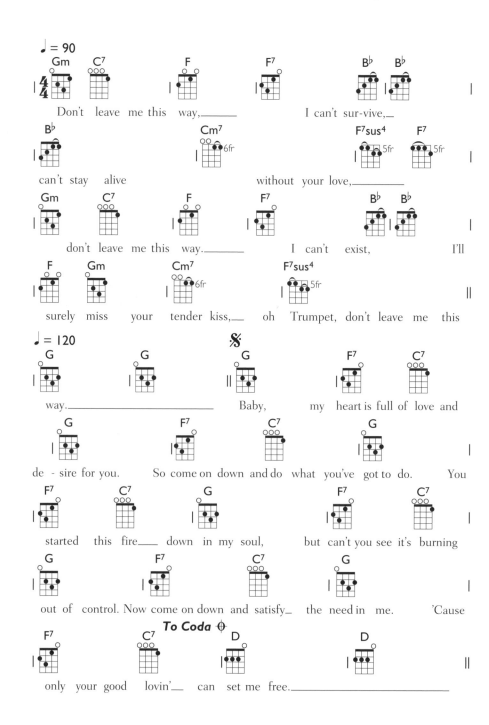

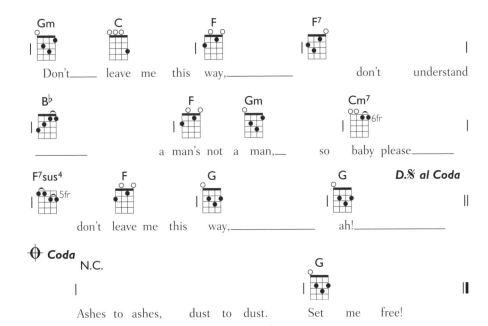

cont.

Gm | C | F | F7

Don't___ leave me this way,_____ don't understand

Bb | F | Gm | Cm7

_____ a man's not a man,__ so baby please_____

F7sus4 | F | G | G **D.%. al Coda**

don't leave me this way,_____ ah!_____

✛ **Coda** N.C.   G

Ashes to ashes, dust to dust. Set me free!

Don't Rain On My Parade

Words by Bob Merrill
Music by Jule Styne

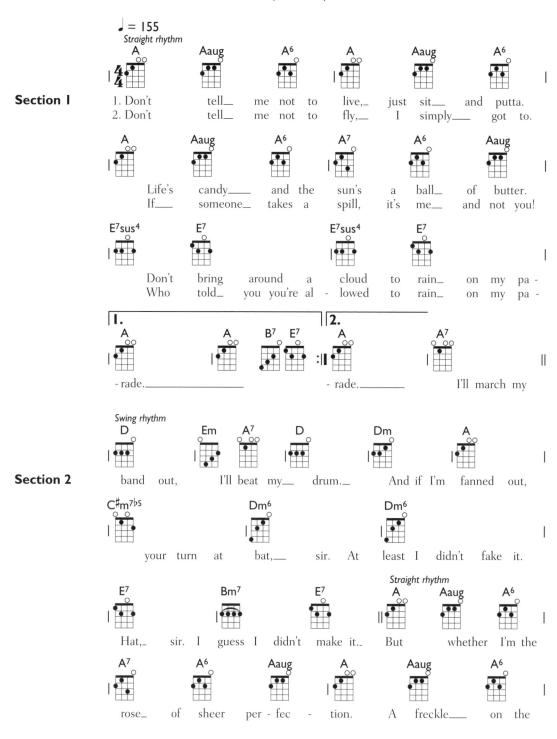

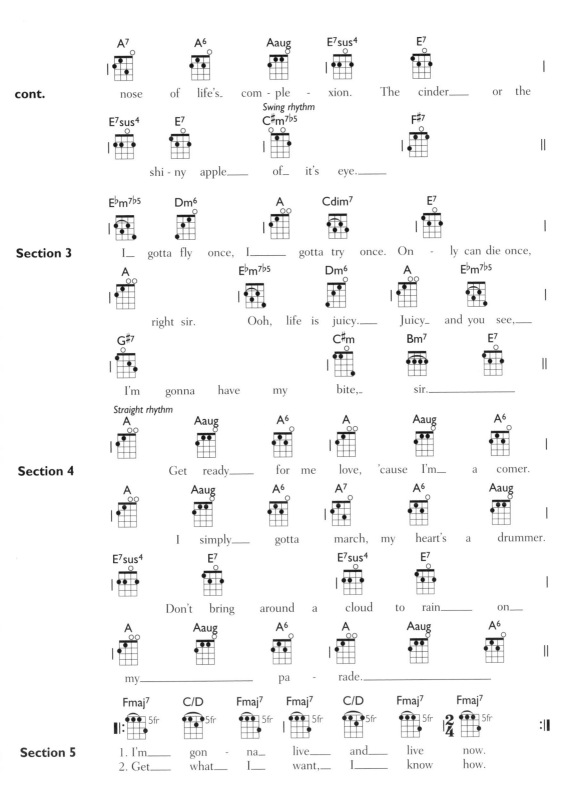

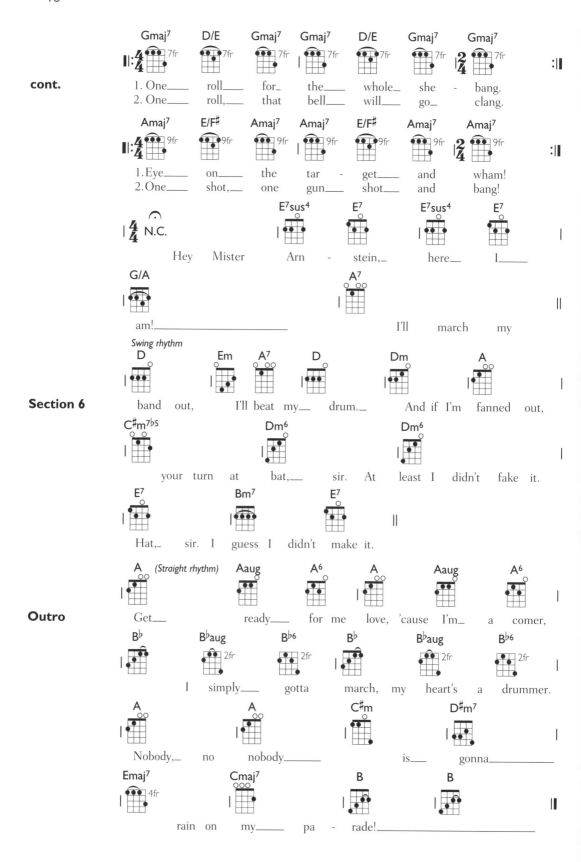

cont.

1. One___ roll___ for_ the___ whole_ she - bang.
2. One___ roll,___ that bell___ will___ go_ clang.

1. Eye___ on___ the tar - get___ and wham!
2. One___ shot,__ one gun___ shot___ and bang!

Hey Mister Arn - stein,_ here_ I____

am!_____ I'll march my

Section 6 band out, I'll beat my__ drum._ And if I'm fanned out,

your turn at bat,__ sir. At least I didn't fake it.

Hat,_ sir. I guess I didn't make it.

Outro Get__ ready___ for me love, 'cause I'm_ a comer,

I simply___ gotta march, my heart's a drummer.

Nobody,_ no nobody_____ is__ gonna_____

rain on my___ pa - rade!_____

Edelweiss

Lyrics by Oscar Hammerstein II
Music by Richard Rodgers

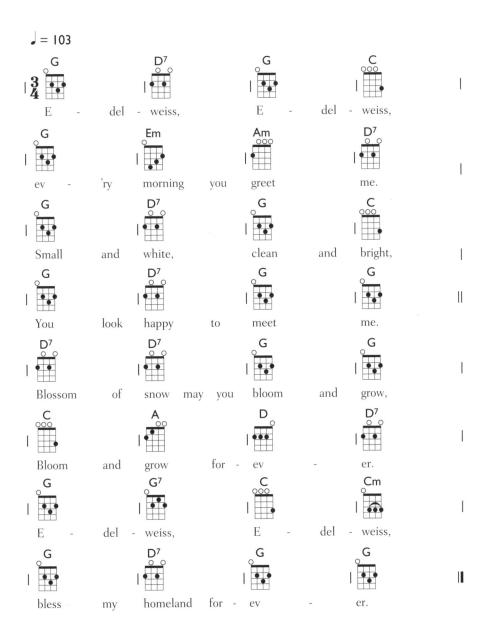

Gigi

Words by Alan Jay Lerner
Music by Frederick Loewe

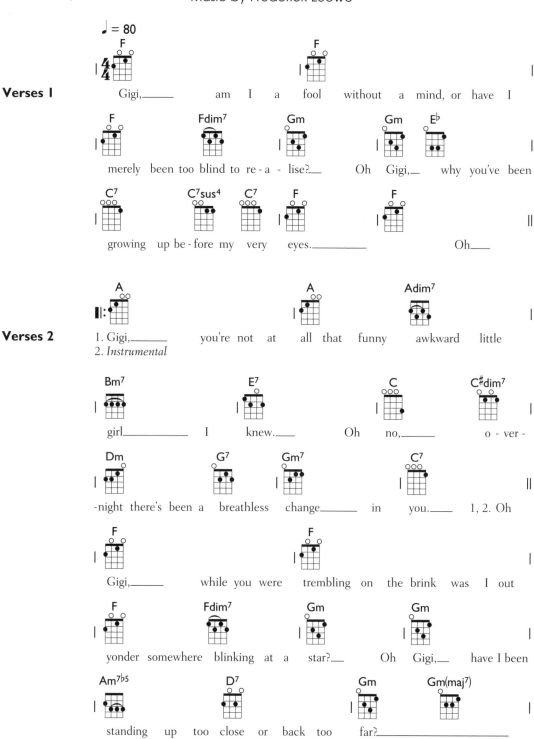

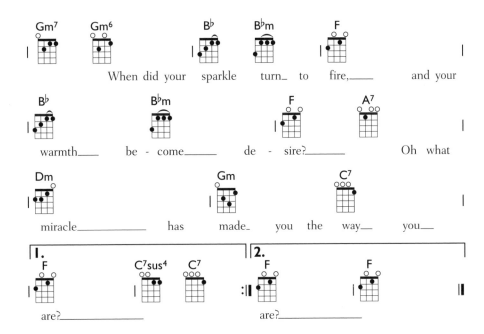

cont.

Gm⁷   Gm⁶   B♭   B♭m   F

When did your   sparkle   turn_ to   fire,___   and your

B♭   B♭m   F   A⁷

warmth___   be - come___   de - sire?___   Oh what

Dm   Gm   C⁷

miracle_____   has   made_   you   the   way_   you_

1.
F   C⁷sus⁴   C⁷   **2.**
F   F

are?_____   are?_____

Hello Dolly

Words and Music by Jerry Herman

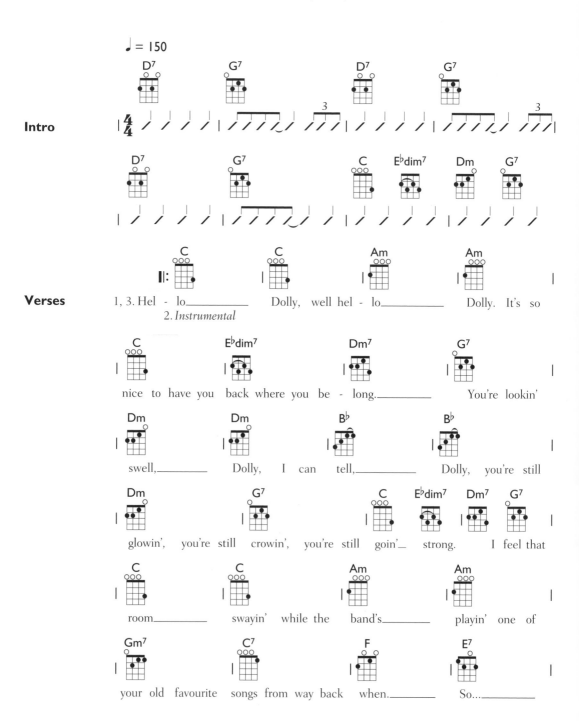

cont.

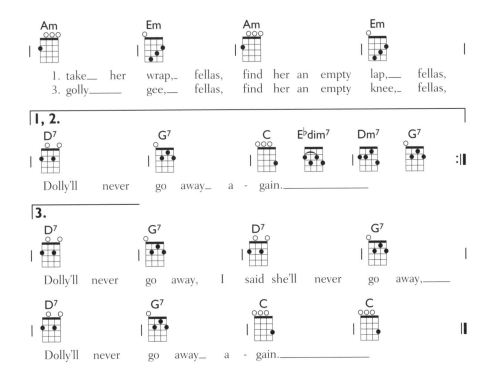

Am	Em	Am	Em
1. take__ her wrap,_	fellas,	find her an empty	lap,__ fellas,
3. golly_____ gee,__	fellas,	find her an empty	knee,_ fellas,

1, 2.

D⁷   G⁷   C   E♭dim⁷   Dm⁷   G⁷

Dolly'll   never   go   away_   a - gain._____

3.

D⁷   G⁷   D⁷   G⁷

Dolly'll   never   go   away,   I   said she'll   never   go   away,____

D⁷   G⁷   C   C

Dolly'll   never   go   away_   a - gain._____

Here I Go Again

Words and Music by David Coverdale and Bernard Marsden

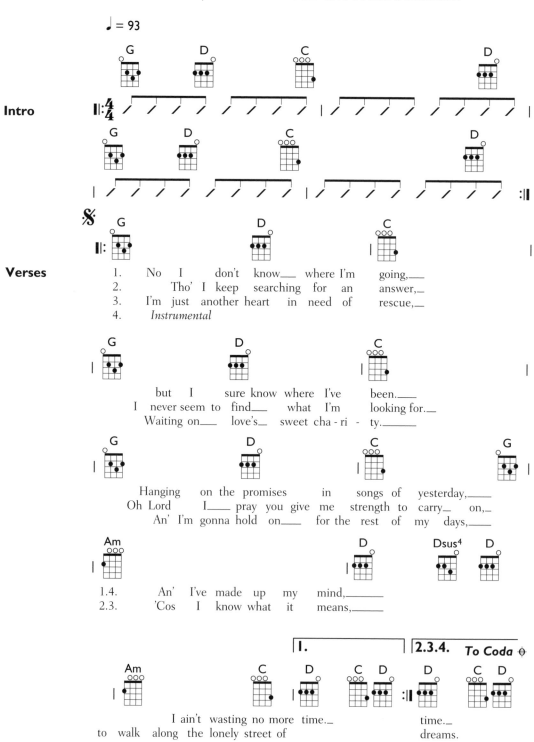

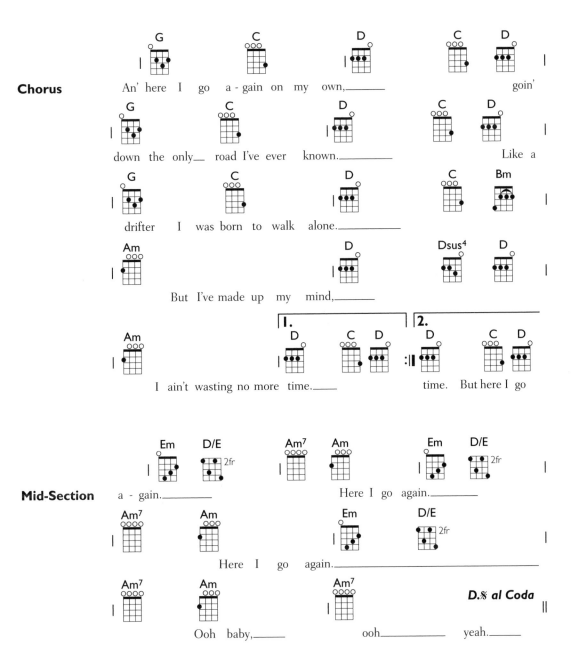

Chorus

G | C | D | C | D |
An' here I go a-gain on my own,_____ goin'

G | C | D | C | D |
down the only__ road I've ever known._____ Like a

G | C | D | C | Bm |
drifter I was born to walk alone._____

Am | D | Dsus⁴ | D |
But I've made up my mind,_____

Am | **1.** D | C | D | **2.** :‖ D | C | D |
I ain't wasting no more time.____ time. But here I go

Mid-Section

Em | D/E | Am⁷ | Am | Em | D/E |
a-gain._____ Here I go again._____

Am⁷ | Am | Em | D/E |
Here I go again._____

Am⁷ | Am | Am⁷ | **D.𝄋 al Coda** ‖
Ooh baby,____ ooh_____ yeah.____

26

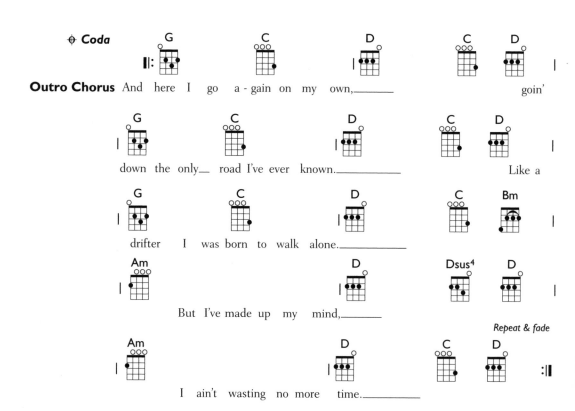

⊕ Coda

Outro Chorus And here I go a-gain on my own,_____ goin'

down the only_ road I've ever known._____ Like a

drifter I was born to walk alone._____

But I've made up my mind,_____

Repeat & fade

I ain't wasting no more time._____

I Am The Very Model Of A
Modern Major General

Words by W.S. Gilbert
Music by Arthur Sullivan

♩ = 200

  C   C

Verses

1. I   am the ve - ry   mo - del of   a   mo - dern Ma - jor Ge - ne - ral, I've
2. I   know our my - thic   his - to - ry, King Ar - thur's and Sir Ca - ra - doc's, I
3. In   fact, when I   know what is meant by "ma - me - lon" and "ra - ve - lin", when

 G⁷   G⁷

in - for - ma - tion ve - ge - ta - ble,   a - ni - mal and mi - ne - ral.   I
an - swer hard a - cros - tics, I've   a   pret - ty taste for pa - ra - dox.   I
I   can tell at sight a Mau - ser   ri - fle from a   ja - ve - lin, when

 C   C

know the kings of Eng - land, and   I   quote the fights his - to - ri - cal, from
quote in e - le - gi - acs all   the   crimes of He - lio - ga - ba - lus, in
such af - fairs as sor - ties and sur - pri - ses I'm more wa - ry   at, and

 G   D⁷   G

Ma - ra - thon to Wa - ter - loo, in   or - der ca - te - go - ri - cal.   I'm
co - nics I   can floor pe - cu - li - a - ri - ties pa - ra - bo - lous. I can
when I   know pre - cise - ly what is   meant by "com - mis - sa - ri - at." When

 G⁷   G⁷   Cm

ve - ry   well   ac - quain - ted, too, with mat - ters ma - the - ma - ti - cal,   I
tell un - doub - ted   Ra - pha - els from Ge - rard Dows and Zof - fa - nies,   I
I have learnt what pro - gress has been made in   mo - dern gun - ne - ry, when

 B♭⁷   B♭⁷   E♭

un - der - stand   e - qua - tions, both the   sim - ple and qua - dra - ti - cal.   A -
know the croak - ing cho - rus   from the   Frogs of   A - ris - to - pha - nes! Then
I   know more   of tac - tics than a   no - vice in   a   nun - ne - ry.   In

 G⁷   G⁷   Cm

-bout   bi - no - mial the - o - rem I'm tee - ming with   a   lot o' news, with
I   can hum a fugue of which I've heard the   mu - sic's din a - fore, and
short, when I've a smat - te - ring of   e - le - men - tal stra - te - gy, you'll

28

cont.

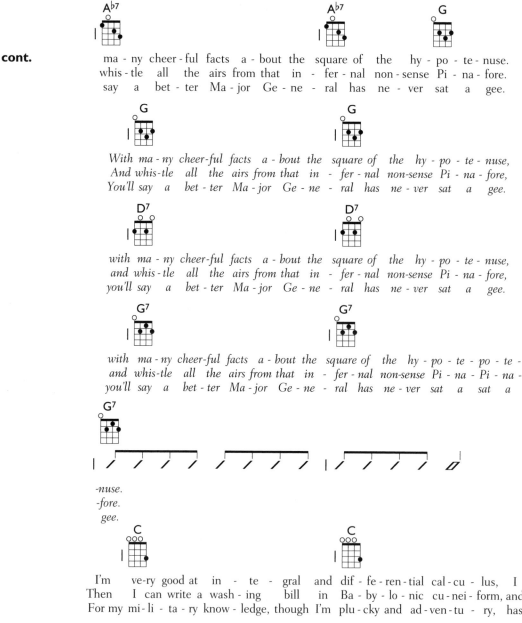

Ab7 Ab7 G

ma - ny cheer - ful facts a - bout the square of the hy - po - te - nuse.
whis - tle all the airs from that in - fer - nal non - sense Pi - na - fore.
say a bet - ter Ma - jor Ge - ne - ral has ne - ver sat a gee.

G G

With ma - ny cheer-ful facts a - bout the square of the hy - po - te - nuse,
And whis-tle all the airs from that in - fer - nal non-sense Pi - na - fore,
You'll say a bet - ter Ma - jor Ge - ne - ral has ne - ver sat a gee.

D7 D7

with ma - ny cheer-ful facts a - bout the square of the hy - po - te - nuse,
and whis-tle all the airs from that in - fer - nal non-sense Pi - na - fore,
you'll say a bet - ter Ma - jor Ge - ne - ral has ne - ver sat a gee.

G7 G7

with ma - ny cheer-ful facts a - bout the square of the hy - po - te - po - te -
and whis-tle all the airs from that in - fer - nal non-sense Pi - na - Pi - na -
you'll say a bet - ter Ma - jor Ge - ne - ral has ne - ver sat a sat a

G7

-nuse.
-fore.
gee.

C C

I'm ve-ry good at in - te - gral and dif - fe - ren - tial cal - cu - lus, I
Then I can write a wash - ing bill in Ba - by - lo - nic cu - nei - form, and
For my mi - li - ta - ry know - ledge, though I'm plu - cky and ad - ven - tu - ry, has

G7 G7

know the sci - en - ti - fic names of be - ings a - ni - mal - cu - lous. In
tell you e - very de - tail of Ca - rac - ta - cus - 's u - ni - form. In
on - ly been brought down to the be - gin - ning of the cen - tu - ry. But

C G7 C G7

short, in mat - ters ve - ge - ta - ble, a - ni - mal and mi - ne - ral, ⎫
short, in mat - ters ve - ge - ta - ble, a - ni - mal and mi - ne - ral, ⎬ I
still, in mat - ters ve - ge - ta - ble, a - ni - mal and mi - ne - ral, ⎭

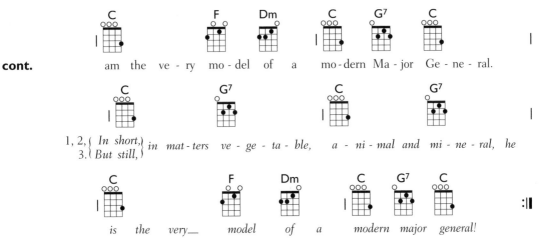

cont. am the ve - ry mo - del of a mo - dern Ma - jor Ge - ne - ral.

1, 2, { In short,}
3. { But still, } in mat - ters ve - ge - ta - ble, a - ni - mal and mi - ne - ral, he

is the very— model of a modern major general!

I Am What I Am

Words and Music by Jerry Herman

31

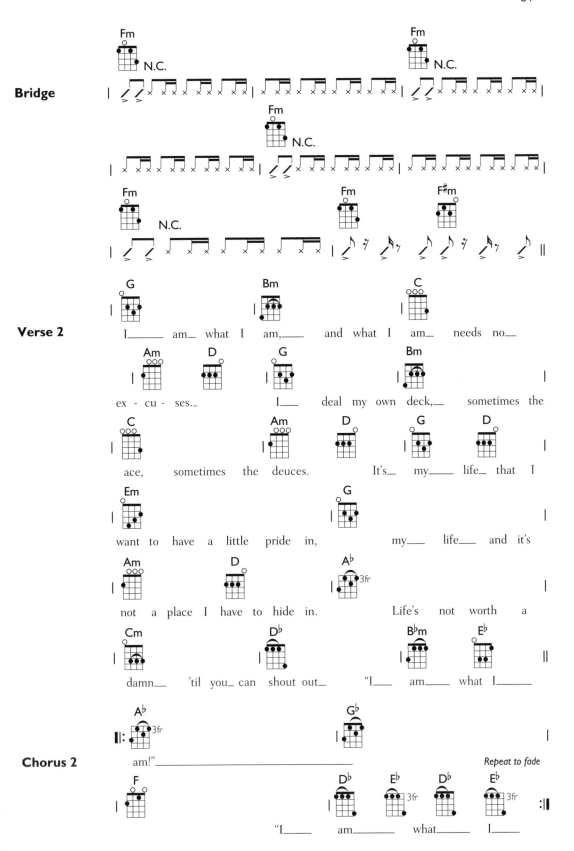

I Get A Kick Out Of You

Words and Music by Cole Porter

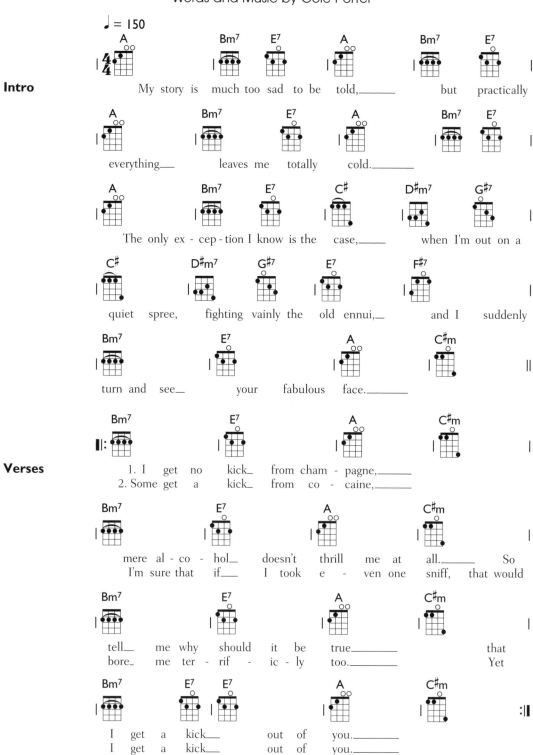

Middle

A⁷	A⁷	D	D	A
I—	get a	kick every	time— I	see— you	standing

A	F#⁷	F#⁷	Bm⁷	Bm⁷
there—	be - fore———	me.—	I— get a	kick, though it's

F#⁷	F#⁷	B⁷	B⁷	E⁷sus⁴	E⁷
clear—	to me,—	you—	obviously—	don't a - dore—	me.—

Chorus

Bm⁷	E⁷	A	C#m
I get no	kick—	in a	plane.———————

Bm⁷	E⁷	C#m⁷	F#m
Flying too	high—	with some guy—	in the sky— is my

Bm⁷ E⁷	Bm⁷ E⁷	C#m⁷ G⁷	F#⁷
i - dea of	no - thing to	do,———————	yet

Bm⁷	E⁷	A	Bm⁷ E⁷ A
I— get a	kick out of	you.———————————————

I Got Plenty O' Nuttin'

Music and Lyrics by George Gershwin, Du Bose Heyward,
Dorothy Heyward and Ira Gershwin

Verses

1. I got plenty o' nuttin',____ and nuttin's plen - ty for
2. I got plenty o' nuttin',____ and nuttin's plen - ty for

me, I got no car, I got no mule, I
me, I got the sun, I got the moon, I

got no mi - se - ry,_____ oh,
got the deep blue sea,_____ oh,

folks with plenty of plenty,_____ got a lock on theie
folks with plenty of plenty,_____ got to pray all the

door, oh, a - fraid some - bo - dy's a going__ to rob 'em while they're
day, oh, seems with plenty__ you sure got to worry how to

out a ma - king more,_____ what for?_____
keep the devil a - way,_____ a - way._____

I got no lock on my door, that's no way to
I ain't__ frettin' 'bout hell 'til the time ar -

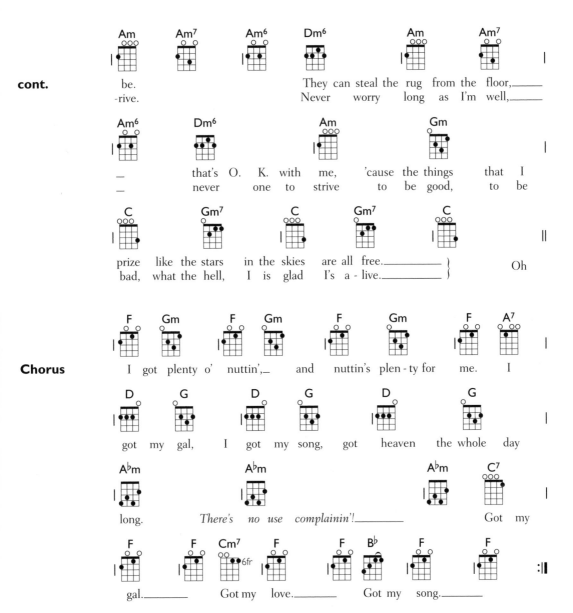

cont.

be. / -rive.

They can steal the rug from the floor,_____
Never worry long as I'm well,_____

_ that's O. K. with me, 'cause the things that I
_ never one to strive to be good, to be

prize like the stars in the skies are all free._____ }
bad, what the hell, I is glad I's a - live._____ }

Oh

Chorus

I got plenty o' nuttin',_ and nuttin's plen - ty for me. I

got my gal, I got my song, got heaven the whole day

long. *There's no use complainin'!*_____ Got my

gal._____ Got my love._____ Got my song._____

I Got Rhythm

Music and Lyrics by George Gershwin and Ira Gershwin

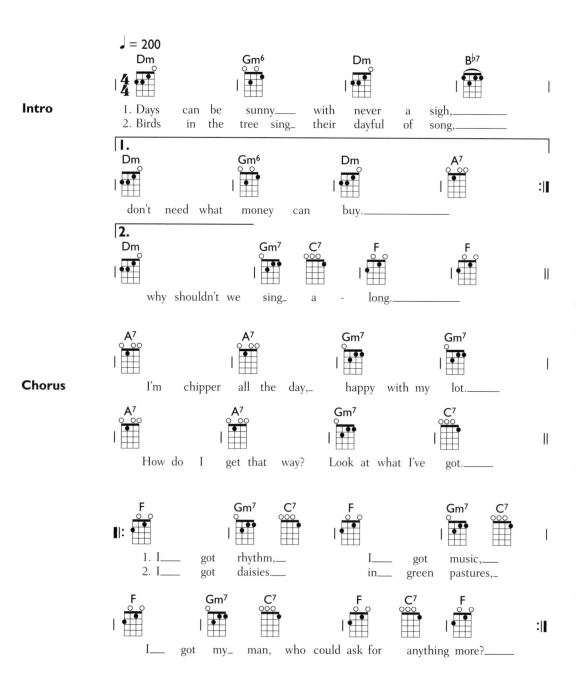

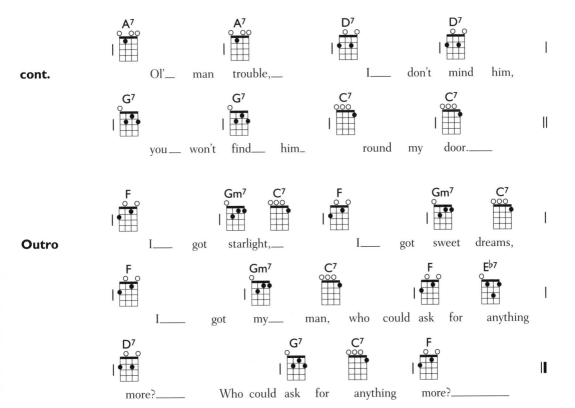

cont.

A⁷	A⁷	D⁷	D⁷
Ol'__ man	trouble,__	I__ don't	mind him,

G⁷	G⁷	C⁷	C⁷
you__ won't	find__ him_	round my	door.____

Outro

F	Gm⁷ C⁷	F	Gm⁷ C⁷
I__ got	starlight,__	I__ got	sweet dreams,

F	Gm⁷ C⁷	F E♭⁷
I____ got	my__ man, who could ask	for anything

D⁷	G⁷ C⁷ F
more?_____	Who could ask for anything more?_____

If I Were A Rich Man

Words by Sheldon Harnick
Music by Jerry Bock

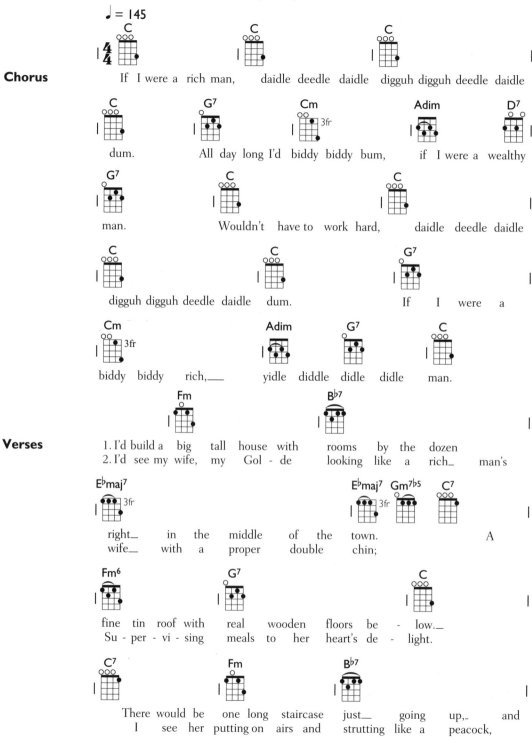

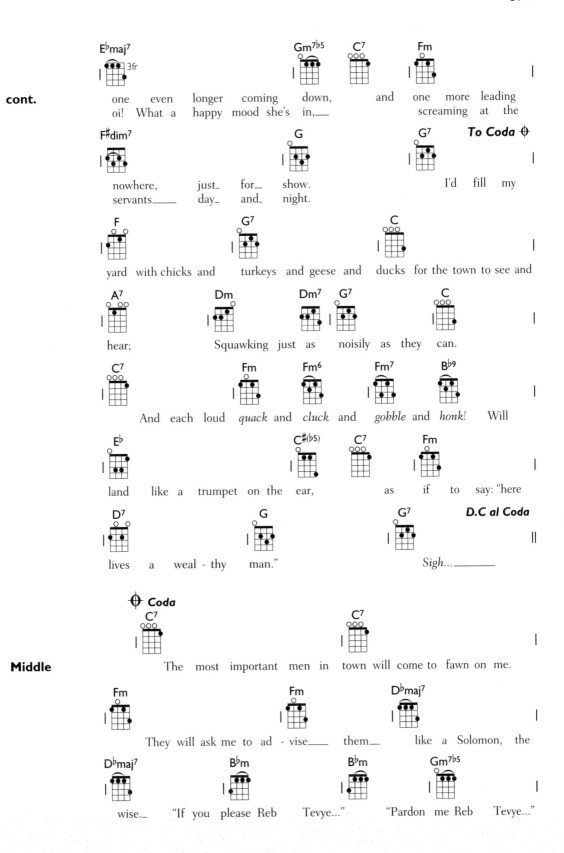

E♭maj⁷ ⟨3fr⟩　　　　　　　Gm⁷♭⁵　　C⁷　　Fm

cont.　　one　even　longer　coming　down,　　and　one　more　leading
　　　　　　oi! What a　happy　mood she's　in,___　　　　screaming　at　the

F♯dim⁷　　　　　　　　　G　　　　　　G⁷　　　***To Coda ⊕***

　　nowhere,　　　just_　for_　show.　　　　　　I'd　fill　my
　　servants___　　day_　and_　night.

F　　　　　　G⁷　　　　　　　　C

　　yard　with chicks and　　turkeys　and geese and　ducks　for the town to see and

A⁷　　　　　Dm　　　　Dm⁷ G⁷　　　　　　C

　　hear;　　　　Squawking just　as　noisily　as　they　can.

C⁷　　　　　　Fm　　　Fm⁶　　　Fm⁷　　B♭⁹

　　And　each　loud　*quack*　and　*cluck*　and　*gobble* and　*honk!*　Will

E♭　　　　　　　　C♯⁽♭⁵⁾　C⁷　　Fm

　　land　like　a　trumpet　on the　ear,　　　as　if　to　say: "here

D⁷　　　　　　G　　　　　　　G⁷　　　***D.C al Coda***

　　lives　a　weal - thy　man."　　　　　　*Sigh...*___

⊕ ***Coda***
　　C⁷　　　　　　　　　　　C⁷

Middle　　The　most　important　men　in　town　will　come　to　fawn　on　me.

Fm　　　　　　　Fm　　　　D♭maj⁷

　　They　will　ask　me　to　ad - vise___　them_　like　a　Solomon,　the

D♭maj⁷　　　　　B♭m　　　　B♭m　　　　Gm⁷♭⁵

　　wise._　"If　you　please Reb　Tevye..."　　"Pardon　me Reb　Tevye..."

40

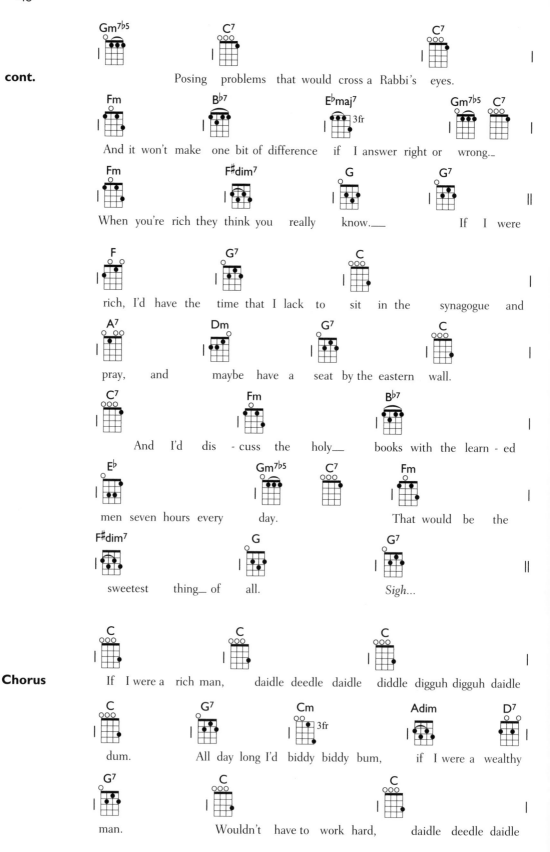

cont.

Gm⁷ᵇ⁵ **C⁷** **C⁷**

Posing problems that would cross a Rabbi's eyes.

Fm **B♭⁷** **E♭maj⁷** 3fr **Gm⁷ᵇ⁵** **C⁷**

And it won't make one bit of difference if I answer right or wrong._

Fm **F♯dim⁷** **G** **G⁷**

When you're rich they think you really know.__ If I were

F **G⁷** **C**

rich, I'd have the time that I lack to sit in the synagogue and

A⁷ **Dm** **G⁷** **C**

pray, and maybe have a seat by the eastern wall.

C⁷ **Fm** **B♭⁷**

And I'd dis - cuss the holy__ books with the learn - ed

E♭ **Gm⁷ᵇ⁵** **C⁷** **Fm**

men seven hours every day. That would be the

F♯dim⁷ **G** **G⁷**

sweetest thing_ of all. *Sigh...*

C **C** **C**

Chorus If I were a rich man, daidle deedle daidle diddle digguh digguh daidle

C **G⁷** **Cm** 3fr **Adim** **D⁷**

dum. All day long I'd biddy biddy bum, if I were a wealthy

G⁷ **C** **C**

man. Wouldn't have to work hard, daidle deedle daidle

Faber Music's Ukulele Song Finder

Are you looking for a particular song arranged specifically for ukulele? This useful alphabetical song finder will help you identify which book contains the song you are looking for. Faber Music publishes a wealth of ukulele books suitable for players from absolute beginner to intermediate level.

The Ukulele Playlist: Yellow Book
ISBN 0-571-53328-0
The Ukulele Rock Playlist: Black Book
ISBN 0-571-53565-8
The Ukulele Playlist: Orange Book
ISBN 0-571-53616-6
The Ukulele Playlist: Christmas
ISBN 0-571-53358-2
The Ukulele Playlist: Blue Book
ISBN 0-571-53327-2
The Ukulele Playlist: White Book
ISBN 0-571-53391-4
The Ukulele Playlist: Red Book
ISBN 0-571-53390-6
The Ukulele Jazz Playlist: Purple Book
ISBN 0-571-53566-6
The Ukulele Playlist: Green Book
ISBN 0-571-53645-X
The Really Easy Uke Book
ISBN 0-571-53374-4
Easy Uke Library: Over The Rainbow
ISBN 0-571-53608-5
Easy Uke Library: Bare Necessities
ISBN 0-571-53606-9
Easy Uke Library: Memory
ISBN 0-571-53607-7
Ukulele Basics
ISBN 0-571-53588-7

FABER 𝆑𝆑 MUSIC

Ukulele Song Finder

1,2,3,4 *The Ukulele Playlist: Green Book*
A Foggy Day *The Ukulele Playlist: Purple Book*
A Sailor Went To Sea *Ukulele Basics*
Ain't Misbehavin' *The Ukulele Playlist: Purple Book*
All Along The Watchtower *The Ukulele Playlist: White Book & The Really Easy Uke Book*
All Day And All Of The Night *The Ukulele Playlist: Black Book*
Aloha Oe *The Ukulele Playlist: Green Book*
Always Look On The Bright Side Of Life *The Ukulele Playlist: Blue Book*
Amazing Grace *The Really Easy Uke Book*
American Idiot *The Ukulele Playlist: Red Book*
Angels *The Ukulele Playlist: White Book*
Angels From The Realms Of Glory *The Ukulele Playlist: Christmas Book*
Anything Goes *The Ukulele Playlist: Green Book*
Auld Lang Syne *The Ukulele Playlist: Christmas Book*
Autumn Leaves *The Ukulele Playlist: Purple Book*
Away In A Manger *The Ukulele Playlist: Christmas Book*
Babooshka *The Ukulele Playlist: Yellow Book*
Back For Good *The Ukulele Playlist: Blue Book*
Back In Black *The Ukulele Playlist: Red Book*
Bad Moon Rising *The Ukulele Playlist: Yellow Book*
Banana Boat Song, The *The Ukulele Playlist: Green Book & Ukulele Basics*
Basket Case *The Ukulele Playlist: Black Book*
Beat It *The Ukulele Playlist: Yellow Book*
Beep Beep Song *The Ukulele Playlist: Yellow Book*
Bewitched *The Ukulele Playlist: Purple Book*
Bill Bailey, Won't You Please Come Home *The Ukulele Playlist: Green Book*
Bittersweet Symphony *The Ukulele Playlist: Blue Book*
Blue Christmas *The Ukulele Playlist: Christmas Book*
Blue Moon *The Ukulele Playlist: White Book & Ukulele Basics*
Boar's Head Carol *The Ukulele Playlist: Christmas Book*
Boulevard Of Broken Dreams *The Ukulele Playlist: Yellow Book*
Breakfast At Tiffany's *The Ukulele Playlist: Yellow Book*
Bright Eyes *The Ukulele Playlist: White Book*
Build Me Up Buttercup *The Ukulele Playlist: Blue Book*
By The Light Of The Silvery Moon *The Ukulele Playlist: Green Book*
Call Me *The Ukulele Playlist: Red Book*
Candy *The Ukulele Playlist: Red Book*
Can't Get You Out Of My Head *The Ukulele Playlist: White Book*
Christmas Song, The (Chestnuts Roasting On An Open Fire) *The Ukulele Playlist: Christmas Book*
Clementine *Ukulele Basics*
Coffee & TV *The Ukulele Playlist: White Book*
Come Away With Me *The Ukulele Playlist: Purple Book*
Come On Eileen *The Ukulele Playlist: Blue Book*
Complicated *The Ukulele Playlist: Orange Book*
Cotton Fields (The Cotton Song) *The Ukulele Playlist: Green Book*
Crazy *The Ukulele Playlist: Yellow Book & The Ukulele Playlist: Orange Book*
Crazy Little Thing Called Love *The Ukulele Playlist: Blue Book*
Creep *The Ukulele Playlist: Blue Book*
Cry Me A River *The Ukulele Playlist: Purple Book*
Daisy Bell *Ukulele Basics*
Dancing In The Moonlight *The Ukulele Playlist: Orange Book*
Danny Boy *The Really Easy Uke Book*
Daydream Believer *The Ukulele Playlist: Blue Book*
Deck The Halls *The Ukulele Playlist: Christmas Book*
Delilah *The Really Easy Uke Book*
Ding Dong Merrily On High *The Ukulele Playlist: Christmas Book*
Dirty Old Town *The Really Easy Uke Book*
Do They Know It's Christmas *The Ukulele Playlist: Christmas Book*
Don't Fence Me In *The Ukulele Playlist: Green Book*
Don't Get Me Wrong *The Ukulele Playlist: Blue Book*

Don't Look Back Into The Sun *The Ukulele Playlist: Black Book*
Don't Stop Believin' *The Ukulele Playlist: Black Book*
Don't Stop Me Now *The Ukulele Playlist: Red Book*
Don't You Want Me *The Ukulele Playlist: White Book*
Down Under *The Ukulele Playlist: White Book*
Dreadlock Holiday *The Ukulele Playlist: Red Book*
Dream A Little Dream Of Me *The Ukulele Playlist: Yellow Book*
Drunken Sailor! *Ukulele Basics*
Early One Morning *The Ukulele Playlist: Green Book & The Really Easy Uke Book*
Easy *The Ukulele Playlist: Red Book*
Edelweiss *The Really Easy Uke Book*
Embraceable You *The Ukulele Playlist: Purple Book*
Ever Fallen In Love With Someone You Shouldn't've *The Ukulele Playlist: Red Book*
Everybody Needs Somebody *The Ukulele Playlist: White Book*
Fairy Tale Of New York *The Ukulele Playlist: Christmas Book*
Faith *The Ukulele Playlist: White Book*
Fame *The Ukulele Playlist: Orange Book*
Fascinating Rhythm *The Ukulele Playlist: Purple Book*
Fear, The *The Ukulele Playlist: Red Book*
Fell In Love With A Girl *The Ukulele Playlist: Red Book*
Fisherman's Blues *The Ukulele Playlist: Yellow Book*
Flagpole Sitta *The Ukulele Playlist: Blue Book*
Fluorescent Adolescent *The Ukulele Playlist: Blue Book*
Foundations *The Ukulele Playlist: Blue Book*
Frankie *The Ukulele Playlist: Orange Book*
Frère Jacques *Ukulele Basics*
From Both Sides Now *The Ukulele Playlist: Green Book*
Frosty The Snowman *The Ukulele Playlist: Christmas Book*
Get It On *The Ukulele Playlist: Black Book*
Get Me To The Church On Time *The Really Easy Uke Book*
Go Your Own Way *The Ukulele Playlist: Blue Book*
Good King Wenceslas *The Ukulele Playlist: Christmas Book*
Grandma Got Run Over By A Reindeer *The Ukulele Playlist: Christmas Book*
Grease *The Ukulele Playlist: Orange Book*
Greased Lightnin' *The Really Easy Uke Book*
Great Balls Of Fire *The Ukulele Playlist: White Book*
Greatest Day *The Ukulele Playlist: White Book*
Green Door, The *The Ukulele Playlist: Green Book*
Grenade *The Ukulele Playlist: Orange Book*
Ha Ha This A Way *The Ukulele Playlist: Green Book*
Happy Birthday To You *The Really Easy Uke Book*
Happy Together *The Ukulele Playlist: Blue Book*
Hark! The Herald Angels Sing *The Ukulele Playlist: Christmas Book*
Have Yourself A Merry Little Christmas *The Ukulele Playlist: Christmas Book*
Here I Go Again *The Ukulele Playlist: Black Book*
Here We Come A-Wassailing *The Ukulele Playlist: Christmas Book*
He's Got The Whole World In His Hands *Ukulele Basics*
Hey There Delilah *The Ukulele Playlist: Red Book*
Higher Ground *The Ukulele Playlist: White Book*
Hippopotamus Song, The *The Really Easy Uke Book*
Hit The Road Jack *The Ukulele Playlist: Blue Book & The Ukulele Playlist: Purple Book*
Holly & The Ivy, The *The Ukulele Playlist: Christmas Book*
Hotel California *The Ukulele Playlist: Blue Book*
Hounds Of Love *The Ukulele Playlist: Black Book*
House Of Fun *The Ukulele Playlist: Blue Book*
House Of The Rising Sun, The *The Ukulele Playlist: Yellow Book & The Really Easy Uke Book*
How Deep Is Your Love *The Ukulele Playlist: Yellow Book*
How Much Is That Doggie In The Window *The Really Easy Uke Book & Ukulele Basics*

Hush *The Ukulele Playlist: Yellow Book*

I Am What I Am *The Ukulele Playlist: Orange Book*

I Can See Clearly Now *The Ukulele Playlist: Red Book*

I Do Like To Be Beside The Seaside *The Really Easy Uke Book*

I Don't Feel Like Dancin' *The Ukulele Playlist: Yellow Book*

I Don't Wanna Dance *The Ukulele Playlist: White Book*

I Got You Babe *The Ukulele Playlist: Red Book*

I Have A Dream *The Really Easy Uke Book*

I Love Rock N Roll *The Ukulele Playlist: Black Book*

I Only Want To Be With You *The Ukulele Playlist: Green Book*

I Saw Mommy Kissing Santa Claus *The Ukulele Playlist: Christmas Book*

I Wanna Be Like You *The Ukulele Playlist: Blue Book, The Really Easy Uke Book & Ukulele Basics*

I Want To Break Free *The Ukulele Playlist: Black Book*

I Wish *The Ukulele Playlist: Yellow Book*

I Wish It Could Be Christmas Every Day *The Ukulele Playlist: Christmas Book*

If I Had A Hammer *The Really Easy Uke Book*

(I'm Gonna Be) 500 Miles *The Ukulele Playlist: Blue Book & Ukulele Basics*

I'm Gonna Sing *Ukulele Basics*

I'm Yours *The Ukulele Playlist: White Book*

In The Bleak Midwinter *The Ukulele Playlist: Christmas Book*

(Is This The Way To) Amarillo *The Ukulele Playlist: White Book & The Really Easy Uke Book*

Is You Is, Or Is You Ain't My Baby *The Ukulele Playlist: Purple Book*

Islands In The Stream *The Ukulele Playlist: White Book*

Isn't She Lovely *The Ukulele Playlist: Blue Book*

It Had To Be You *The Ukulele Playlist: Purple Book*

It's A Hard Knock Life *The Ukulele Playlist: Green Book*

It's A Long Way To Tipperary *The Ukulele Playlist: Green Book*

I've Got My Love To Keep Me Warm *The Ukulele Playlist: Green Book*

JCB *The Ukulele Playlist: Orange Book*

Jean Genie, The *The Ukulele Playlist: Black Book*

Jenny Don't Be Hasty *The Ukulele Playlist: White Book*

Jingle Bells *The Ukulele Playlist: Christmas Book*

Jive Talkin' *The Ukulele Playlist: Red Book*

Joy To The World *The Ukulele Playlist: Christmas Book*

Karma Chameleon *The Ukulele Playlist: Red Book*

Kids In America *The Ukulele Playlist: Blue Book*

King Of The Road *The Ukulele Playlist: Yellow Book*

Kiss Me *The Ukulele Playlist: Orange Book*

Knees Up Mother Brown *The Really Easy Uke Book*

Kum-Ba-Yah *The Really Easy Uke Book*

Ku-U-I-Po *The Ukulele Playlist: Green Book*

Last Christmas *The Ukulele Playlist: Christmas Book*

Last Nite *The Ukulele Playlist: Blue Book & The Ukulele Playlist: Black Book*

Let There Be Love *The Ukulele Playlist: Purple Book*

Let's Call The Whole Thing Off *The Ukulele Playlist: Purple Book*

Let's Face The Music And Dance *The Ukulele Playlist: Purple Book*

Life On Mars? *The Ukulele Playlist: Yellow Book*

Like A Prayer *The Ukulele Playlist: Yellow Book*

Lithium *The Ukulele Playlist: Black Book*

Little Brown Jug *The Really Easy Uke Book*

Little Drummer Boy, The *The Ukulele Playlist: Christmas Book*

Live And Let Die *The Ukulele Playlist: Black Book*

Living Doll *The Ukulele Playlist: White Book*

Look Of Love, The *The Ukulele Playlist: Purple Book*

Losing My Religion *The Ukulele Playlist: Yellow Book*

Love Is A Losing Game *The Ukulele Playlist: Red Book*

Love Is In The Air *The Ukulele Playlist: Orange Book*

Love Machine *The Ukulele Playlist: Orange Book*

Lucky *The Ukulele Playlist: Black Book*

Lullaby Of Birdland *The Ukulele Playlist: Purple Book*

Mack The Knife *The Ukulele Playlist: Red Book*

Mad About The Boy *The Ukulele Playlist: Purple Book*

Making Plans For Nigel *The Ukulele Playlist: Red Book*

Mamma Mia *The Ukulele Playlist: Yellow Book*

Man Who Sold The World, The *The Ukulele Playlist: Blue Book*

Material Girl *The Ukulele Playlist: White Book*

Merry Christmas Everyone *The Ukulele Playlist: Christmas Book*

Merry Xmas Everybody *The Ukulele Playlist: Christmas Book*

Mmmbop *The Ukulele Playlist: Red Book*

Monster *The Ukulele Playlist: Black Book*

Moondance *The Ukulele Playlist: Purple Book*

More Than A Woman *The Ukulele Playlist: Orange Book*

My Baby Just Cares For Me *The Ukulele Playlist: White Book & The Ukulele Playlist: Purple Book*

My Funny Valentine *The Ukulele Playlist: Purple Book*

My Girl *The Ukulele Playlist: Red Book*

My Grandfather's Clock *The Really Easy Uke Book*

My Sharona *The Ukulele Playlist: Black Book*

My Way *The Ukulele Playlist: Red Book*

Never Want To Say It's Love *The Ukulele Playlist: Blue Book*

No Surprises *The Ukulele Playlist: Red Book*

Nutbush City Limits *The Ukulele Playlist: Blue Book*

O Come All Ye Faithful *The Ukulele Playlist: Christmas Book*

O Holy Night *The Ukulele Playlist: Christmas Book*

On The Street Where You Live *The Ukulele Playlist: Green Book*

Over The Rainbow *The Really Easy Uke Book*

Panic *The Ukulele Playlist: Yellow Book*

Paranoid *The Ukulele Playlist: Yellow Book & The Ukulele Playlist: Black Book*

Passenger, The *The Ukulele Playlist: Blue Book*

Patience *The Ukulele Playlist: Orange Book*

Perfect Day *The Ukulele Playlist: White Book*

Please Don't Let Me Go *The Ukulele Playlist: Orange Book*

Power Of Love, The *The Ukulele Playlist: Orange Book*

Price Tag *The Ukulele Playlist: Green Book*

Promise This *The Ukulele Playlist: Orange Book*

Proud Mary *The Really Easy Uke Book*

Raindrops Keep Falling On My Head *The Ukulele Playlist: White Book*

Real Wild Child (Wild One) *The Ukulele Playlist: Black Book*

Rebel Yell *The Ukulele Playlist: Black Book & The Ukulele Playlist: Red Book*

Rehab *The Ukulele Playlist: Yellow Book*

Rhythm Of Love *The Ukulele Playlist: Orange Book*

Ring Of Fire *The Ukulele Playlist: Yellow Book*

Rock Around The Clock *The Really Easy Uke Book*

Rock DJ *The Ukulele Playlist: Black Book*

Rockin' All Over The World *The Ukulele Playlist: Black Book*

Rockin' Around The Christmas Tree *The Ukulele Playlist: Christmas Book*

Rockin' Robin *The Ukulele Playlist: Green Book*

Rockstar *The Ukulele Playlist: Yellow Book & The Ukulele Playlist: Black Book*

Row, Row, Row Your Boat *Ukulele Basics*

Rudolph The Red Nosed Reindeer *The Ukulele Playlist: Christmas Book*

Run Rudolph Run *The Ukulele Playlist: Christmas Book*

Sail Us Away *Ukulele Basics*

Santa Claus Is Comin' To Town *The Ukulele Playlist: Christmas Book*

Save All Your Kisses For Me *The Ukulele Playlist: Red Book*

School's Out *The Ukulele Playlist: Black Book*

Senses Working Overtime *The Ukulele Playlist: Black Book*

Sex And Drugs And Rock And Roll *The Ukulele Playlist: White Book*

Shake, Rattle & Roll *The Really Easy Uke Book*

Sheena Is A Punk Rocker *The Ukulele Playlist: Black Book*

She'll Be Coming 'Round The Mountain *Ukulele Basics*

Shoop Shoop Song (It's In His Kiss) *The Really Easy Uke Book*

Signed, Sealed, Delivered *The Ukulele Playlist: Yellow Book*

Silent Night *The Ukulele Playlist: Christmas Book*

Skye Boat Song, The *The Really Easy Uke Book*

Sleigh Ride *The Ukulele Playlist: Christmas Book*

Sloop John B *The Ukulele Playlist: Red Book*

Slow Hand *The Ukulele Playlist: Orange Book*

To purchase any of these books, please visit your local music shop,
or alternatively go to **www.fabermusicstore.com** for
a complete listing of our ukulele publications.

FABER *ff* MUSIC

fabermusic.com

cont.

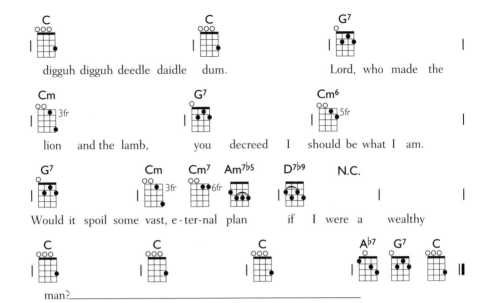

C	C	G⁷
digguh digguh deedle daidle dum.		Lord, who made the

Cm	G⁷	Cm⁶
lion and the lamb,	you decreed I	should be what I am.

G⁷	Cm	Cm⁷	Am⁷♭⁵	D⁷♭⁹	N.C.
Would it spoil some vast, e-ter-nal plan				if I were a	wealthy

C	C	C	A♭⁷	G⁷	C
man?_____					

The Impossible Dream

Words by Joe Darion
Music by Mitch Leigh

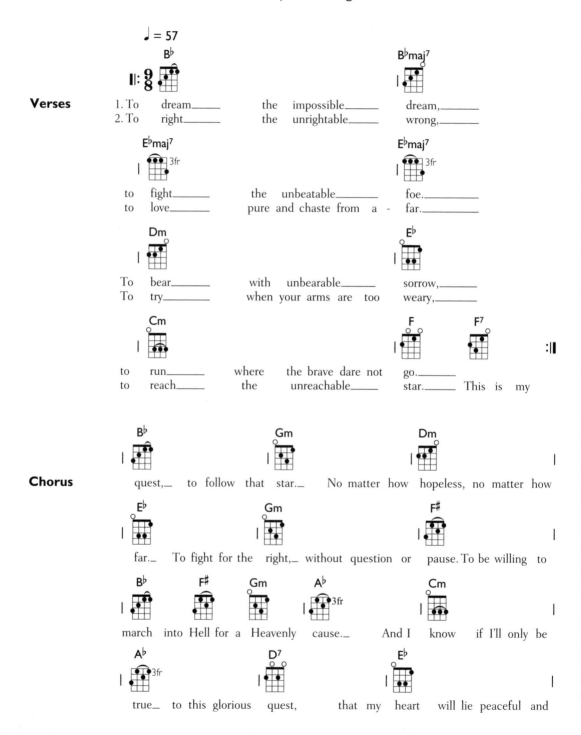

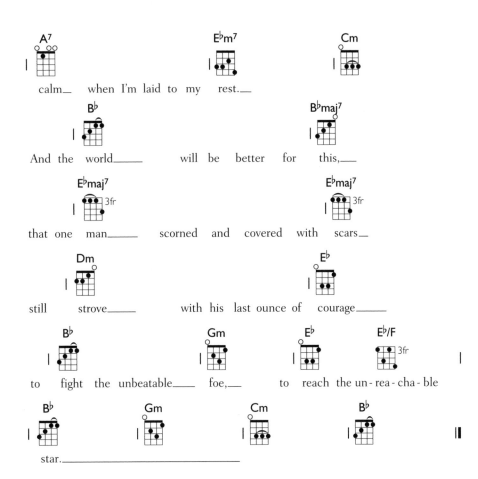

cont.

calm___ when I'm laid to my rest.___

And the world_____ will be better for this,___

that one man_____ scorned and covered with scars___

still strove_____ with his last ounce of courage_____

to fight the unbeatable_____ foe,___ to reach the un‑rea‑cha‑ble

star._____

Losing My Mind

Words and Music by Stephen Sondheim

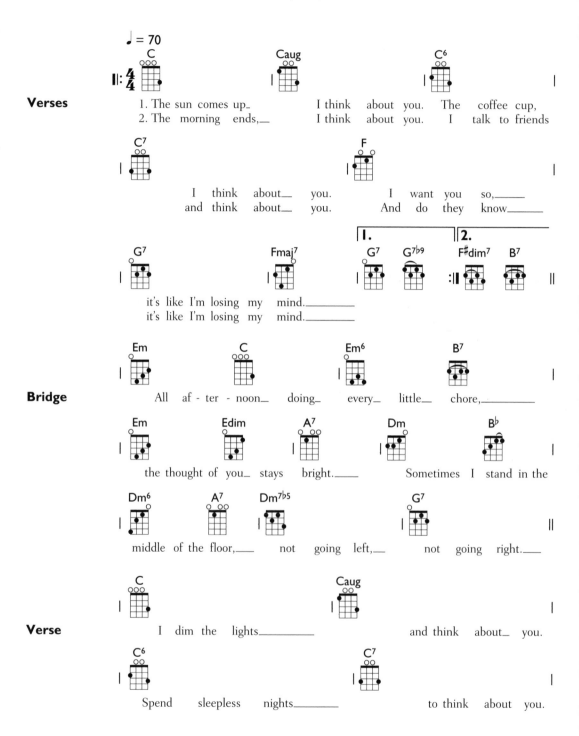

♩ = 70

Verses

C — Caug — C⁶

1. The sun comes up_   I think about you. The coffee cup,
2. The morning ends,_   I think about you. I talk to friends

C⁷ — F

I think about_ you.   I want you so,_____
and think about_ you.   And do they know_____

G⁷ — Fmaj⁷ — **1.** G⁷ G⁷♭⁹ — **2.** F♯dim⁷ B⁷

it's like I'm losing my mind._____
it's like I'm losing my mind._____

Bridge

Em — C — Em⁶ — B⁷

All af-ter-noon_ doing_ every_ little_ chore,_____

Em — Edim — A⁷ — Dm — B♭

the thought of you_ stays bright._____ Sometimes I stand in the

Dm⁶ — A⁷ — Dm⁷♭⁵ — G⁷

middle of the floor,_____ not going left,_ not going right._____

Verse

C — Caug

I dim the lights_____ and think about_ you.

C⁶ — C⁷

Spend sleepless nights_____ to think about you.

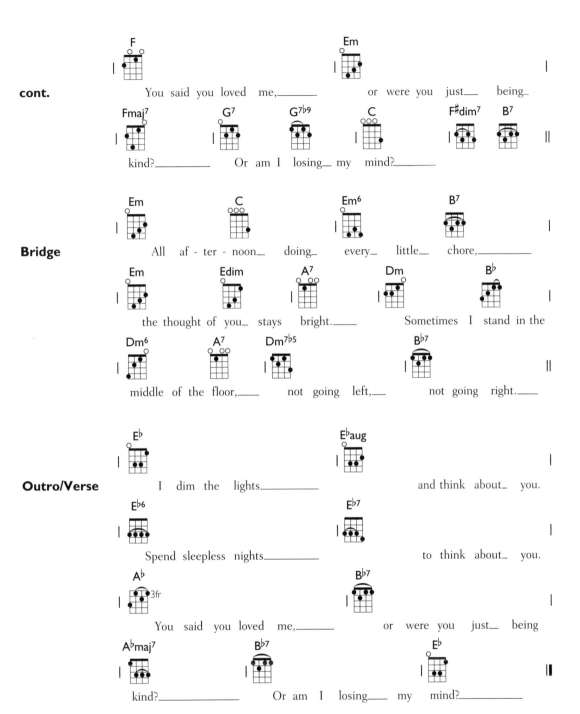

cont.

F — You said you loved me,_____ or were you just__ being__

Fmaj7 G7 G7b9 C F#dim7 B7 — kind?_____ Or am I losing__ my mind?_____

Bridge

Em C Em6 B7 — All af - ter - noon__ doing__ every__ little__ chore,_____

Em Edim A7 Dm Bb — the thought of you__ stays bright.____ Sometimes I stand in the

Dm6 A7 Dm7b5 Bb7 — middle of the floor,____ not going left,__ not going right.____

Outro/Verse

Eb Ebaug — I dim the lights_____ and think about__ you.

Eb6 Eb7 — Spend sleepless nights_____ to think about__ you.

Ab Bb7 — You said you loved me,_____ or were you just__ being

Abmaj7 Bb7 Eb — kind?_____ Or am I losing__ my mind?_____

Love Changes Everything

Text by Don Black and Charles Hart
Music by Andrew Lloyd Webber

47

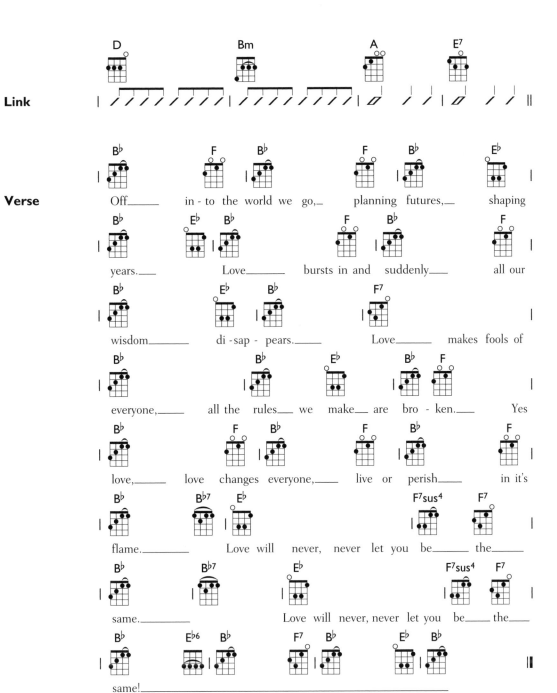

Link

Verse

Off_____ in - to the world we go,_ planning futures,_ shaping

years._ Love_____ bursts in and suddenly_ all our

wisdom_____ di -sap - pears._ Love_____ makes fools of

everyone,_ all the rules_ we make_ are bro - ken._ Yes

love,_ love changes everyone,_ live or perish_ in it's

flame._ Love will never, never let you be_ the_

same._ Love will never, never let you be_ the_

same!_____

Let's Do It (Let's Fall In Love)

Words and Music by Cole Porter

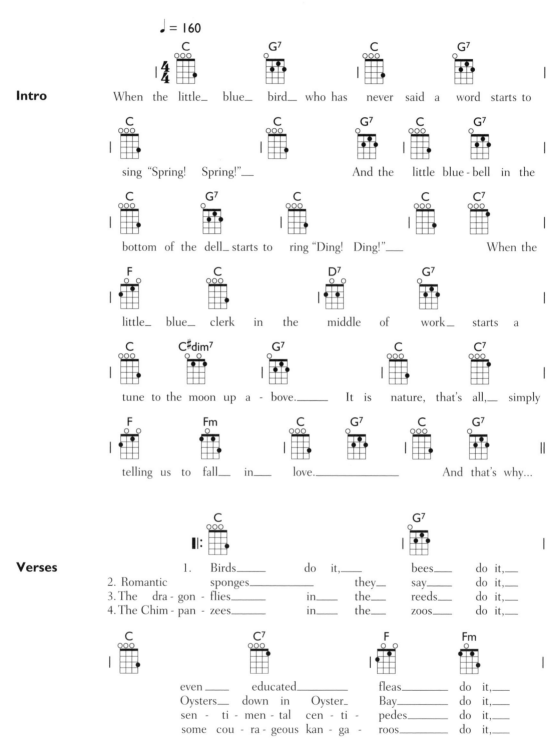

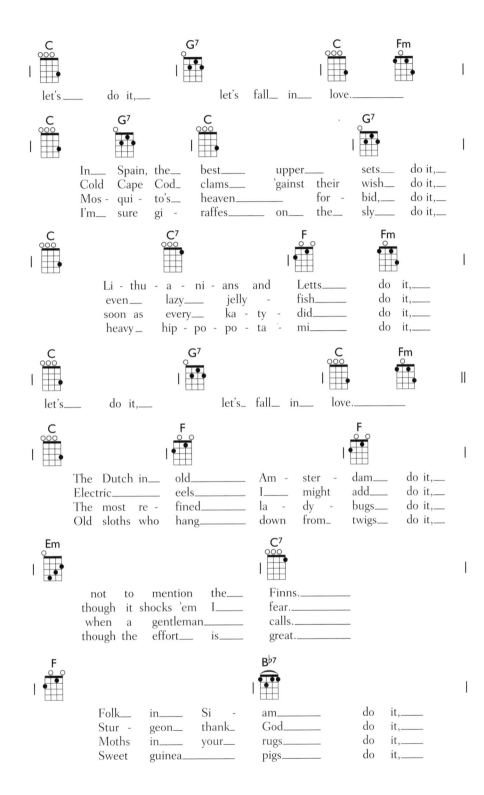

cont. let's ___ do it, ___   let's fall ___ in ___ love. _____

In ___ Spain, the ___ best ___ upper ___ sets ___ do it, ___
Cold Cape Cod_ clams ___ 'gainst their wish ___ do it, ___
Mos - qui - to's_ heaven _____ for - bid, ___ do it, ___
I'm _ sure gi - raffes _____ on ___ the _ sly ___ do it, ___

Li - thu - a - ni - ans and Letts ___ do it, ___
even _ lazy ___ jelly - fish ___ do it, ___
soon as every ___ ka - ty - did ___ do it, ___
heavy _ hip - po - po - ta - mi ___ do it, ___

let's ___ do it, ___   let's_ fall _ in ___ love. _____

The Dutch in _ old _____ Am - ster - dam ___ do it, ___
Electric _____ eels _____ I ___ might add ___ do it, ___
The most re - fined _____ la - dy - bugs ___ do it, ___
Old sloths who hang _____ down from _ twigs ___ do it, ___

not to mention the ___ Finns. _____
though it shocks 'em I ___ fear. _____
when a gentleman _____ calls. _____
though the effort ___ is ___ great. _____

Folk _ in ___ Si - am _____ do it, ___
Stur - geon _ thank_ God _____ do it, ___
Moths in ___ your _ rugs _____ do it, ___
Sweet guinea _____ pigs _____ do it, ___

50

Eb

think of   Siamese_____ twins.. Some_ Ar - gen -
have some caviar_____ dear._ In____ shallow_____
what's the use of moth_ balls?_ Locusts_____ in____
buy   a   couple and__ wait._ We___ know_ that__

C

- tines_____ without_____ means_____ do it,___
shoals,_____ English_____ soles_____ do it,___
trees_____ do   it,___ bees_ do it,___
bears_____ in____ their_ pits_____ do it,___

G7

C   C7   F   Fm

people say in Boston even_ beans_____ do it,___
goldfish in the privacy____ of bowls_____ do it,___
even_ educated_____ fleas_____ do it,___
even_ Pe - ki - ne - ses at the Ritz_____ do it,___

|1-3.| |4.|

C   Am   Dm7b5 G7   C   F   C   G7   C

let's__   do it,__   let's fall in_ love!__

Memory

Music by Andrew Lloyd Webber
Text by Trevor Nunn after T S Eliot

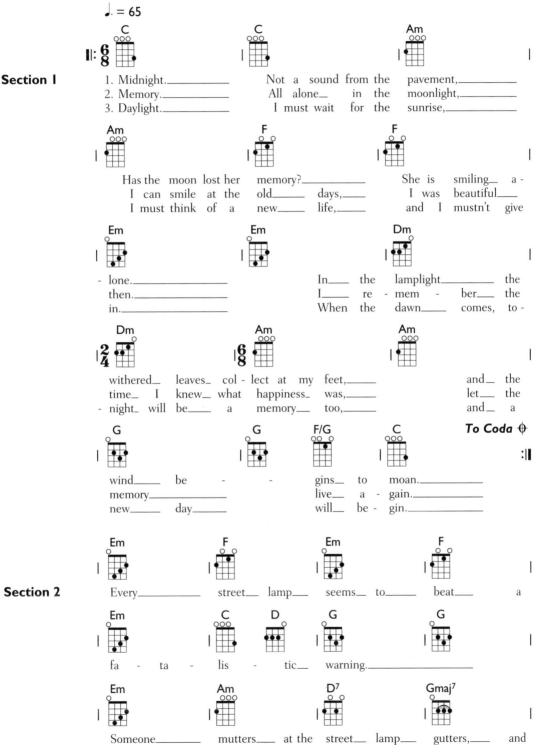

52

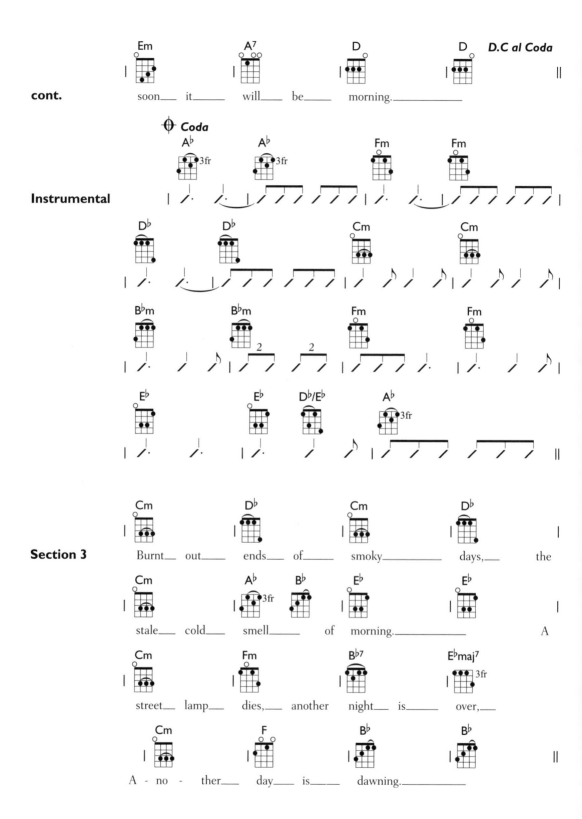

cont.

| Em | A⁷ | D | D *D.C al Coda* |
soon___ it___ will___ be___ morning._____

Instrumental

Coda

Ab | Ab | Fm | Fm

Db | Db | Cm | Cm

Bbm | Bbm | Fm | Fm

Eb | Eb Db/Eb | Ab

Section 3

| Cm | Db | Cm | Db |
Burnt___ out___ ends___ of___ smoky_____ days,___ the

| Cm | Ab Bb | Eb | Eb |
stale___ cold___ smell_____ of morning._____ A

| Cm | Fm | Bb⁷ | Ebmaj⁷ |
street___ lamp___ dies,___ another night___ is___ over,___

| Cm | F | Bb | Bb |
A - no - ther___ day___ is___ dawning._____

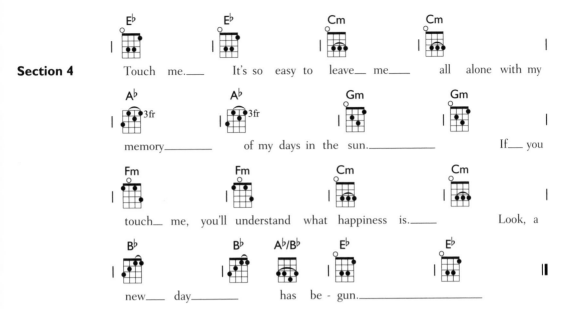

Section 4

E♭	E♭	Cm	Cm	

Touch me.___ It's so easy to leave__ me___ all alone with my

A♭ 3fr	A♭ 3fr	Gm	Gm	

memory_____ of my days in the sun._____ If__ you

Fm	Fm	Cm	Cm	

touch__ me, you'll understand what happiness is.___ Look, a

B♭	B♭	A♭/B♭ E♭	E♭	

new___ day_____ has be - gun._____

Maybe This Time

Words by Fred Ebb
Music by John Kander

Verses

1. Maybe this time,___ I'll be lucky,___
2. Everybody___ loves a winner,___

maybe this time he'll stay.___ Maybe this time,___
so nobody___ loves me.___ Lady___ peaceful,___

for the first time,___ love won't hurry___ a - way.___
Lady___ happy,___ that's what I long to be.___

1.

He will hold me___ fast,___ I'll be home at___

last.___ Not a loser___ anymore,___ like the

last___ time___ and___ the___ time___ be - fore.___

2.

All___ the odds___ are,___ they're in my favour,___

something's bound to be - gin.___ It's gotta happen,___

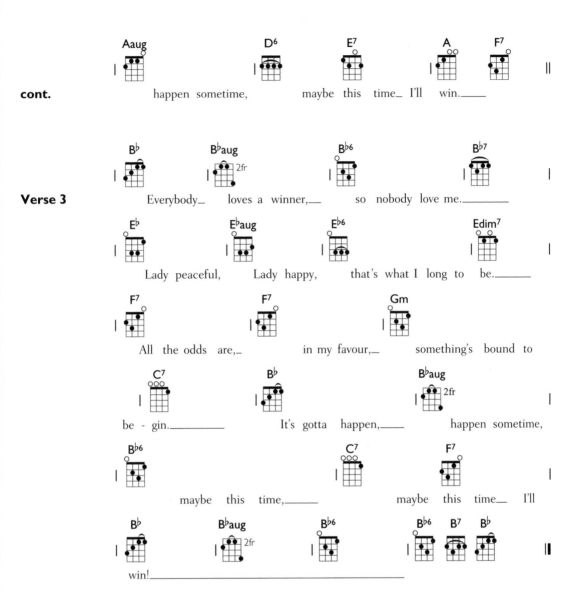

cont.   happen sometime,   maybe this time_ I'll win._

Verse 3   Everybody_ loves a winner,__ so nobody love me._____

Lady peaceful, Lady happy, that's what I long to be._____

All the odds are,_ in my favour,_ something's bound to

be - gin._____ It's gotta happen,____ happen sometime,

maybe this time,_____ maybe this time_ I'll

win!_____

Oh, What A Beautiful Morning

Words by Oscar Hammerstein II
Music by Richard Rodgers

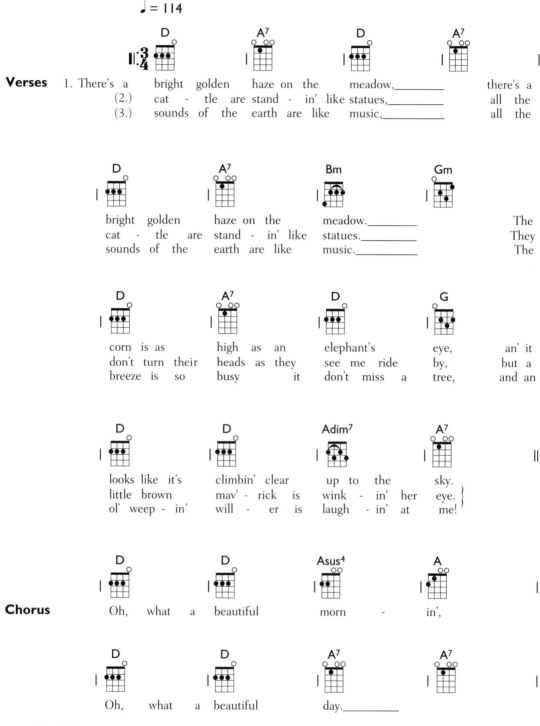

♩ = 114

Verses

1. There's a bright golden haze on the meadow,_____ there's a
(2.) cat - tle are stand - in' like statues,_____ all the
(3.) sounds of the earth are like music,_____ all the

bright golden haze on the meadow._____ The
cat - tle are stand - in' like statues._____ They
sounds of the earth are like music._____ The

corn is as high as an elephant's eye, an' it
don't turn their heads as they see me ride by, but a
breeze is so busy it don't miss a tree, and an

looks like it's climbin' clear up to the sky.
little brown mav' - rick is wink - in' her eye.
ol' weep - in' will - er is laugh - in' at me!

Chorus

Oh, what a beautiful morn - in',

Oh, what a beautiful day._____

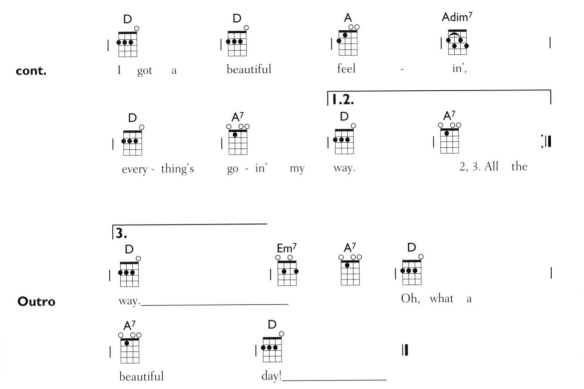

cont.

D · · · ○   D · · · ○   A   Adim⁷

I got a   beautiful   feel - in',

1.2.

D   A⁷   D   A⁷

every - thing's   go - in' my   way.   2, 3. All the

3.

Outro

D   Em⁷   A⁷   D

way._____   Oh, what a

A⁷   D

beautiful   day!_____

On The Street Where You Live

Words by Alan Jay Lerner
Music by Frederick Loewe

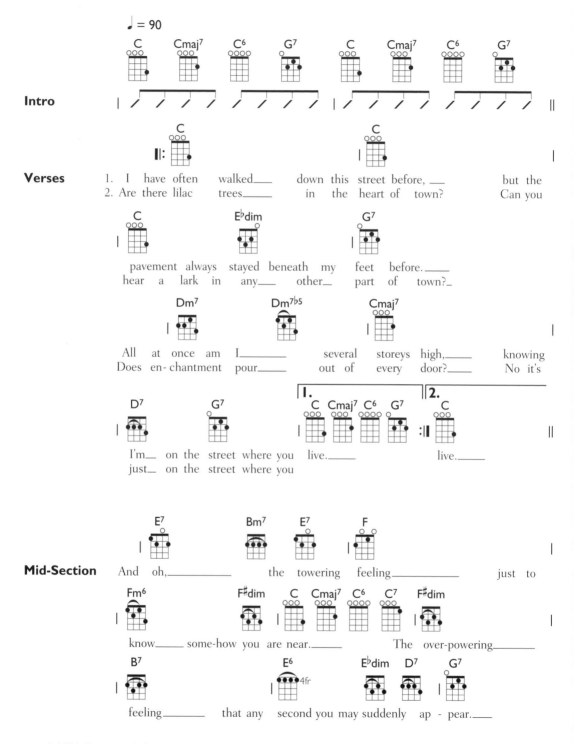

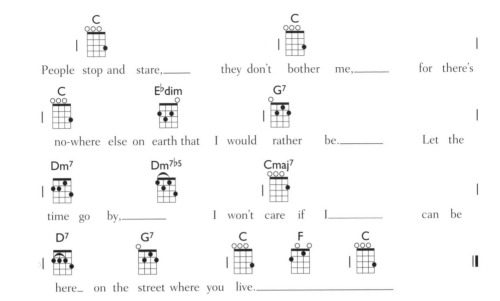

Verse 3

People stop and stare,_____ they don't bother me,_____ for there's

no-where else on earth that I would rather be._____ Let the

time go by,_____ I won't care if I_____ can be

here_ on the street where you live._____

Razzle Dazzle

Words by Fred Ebb
Music by John Kander

♩ = 120

Verses

| G | | | | G | Bᵇdim⁷ | |

Give 'em___ the old_____ razzle_____ dazzle,_____
Give 'em___ the old_____ razzle_____ dazzle,_____

| D⁷ | | D⁷ | | D⁷ | |

razzle dazzle 'em._ Give 'em an act___ with
razzle dazzle 'em._ Give 'em a show that's

| D⁷ | D♯dim⁷ | Em | A⁷ |

lots___ of flash___ in it,___ and the___ re - ac - tion___
so___ splen - di - fe - rous,_ row after_____ row___ will___

| D⁷ | N.C. | G | G | Bᵇdim⁷ |

will___ be passionate.___ Give 'em the old_____ hocus___ pocus,___
grow___ vociferous._____ Give 'em the old_____ flim flam flummox,

| D⁷ | | D⁷ | G⁷ |

bead and feather 'em. How can they see with
fool and fracture 'em. How can they hear the_

| G⁷ | | Cmaj⁷ | C⁶ | Cmaj⁷ | C⁶ |

sequins_____ in___ their_ eyes?_____
truth above_____ the__ roar?_____

| C | | Am⁷ᵇ⁵ | |

What if___ your hinges_____ all___ are___ rusting?_____
Throw 'em___ a fake___ and__ a_____ finagle,_____

| G | N.C. | A⁹ | |

What if,___ in fact,__ you're just___ disgusting?_____
they'll never_____ know_ you're just___ a bagel._____

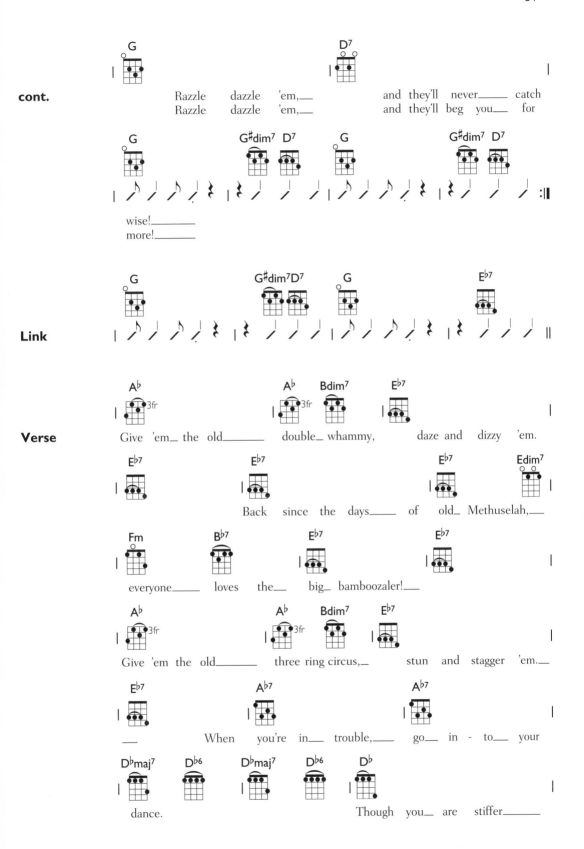

cont.

G   D⁷

Razzle   dazzle   'em,___   and they'll   never____ catch
Razzle   dazzle   'em,___   and they'll   beg   you___ for

G   G#dim⁷ D⁷   G   G#dim⁷ D⁷

wise!_____
more!_____

Link

G   G#dim⁷D⁷   G   E♭⁷

Verse

A♭   A♭   Bdim⁷   E♭⁷

Give 'em_ the old_____ double_ whammy,   daze and dizzy 'em.

E♭⁷   E♭⁷   E♭⁷   Edim⁷

Back   since   the   days____ of   old_ Methuselah,___

Fm   B♭⁷   E♭⁷   E♭⁷

everyone_____ loves   the_   big_ bamboozaler!___

A♭   A♭   Bdim⁷   E♭⁷

Give 'em the old_____ three ring circus,___   stun   and stagger 'em._

E♭⁷   A♭⁷   A♭⁷

___   When   you're in__ trouble,___   go__ in - to__ your

D♭maj⁷   D♭6   D♭maj⁷   D♭6   D♭

dance.   Though you_ are   stiffer_____

62

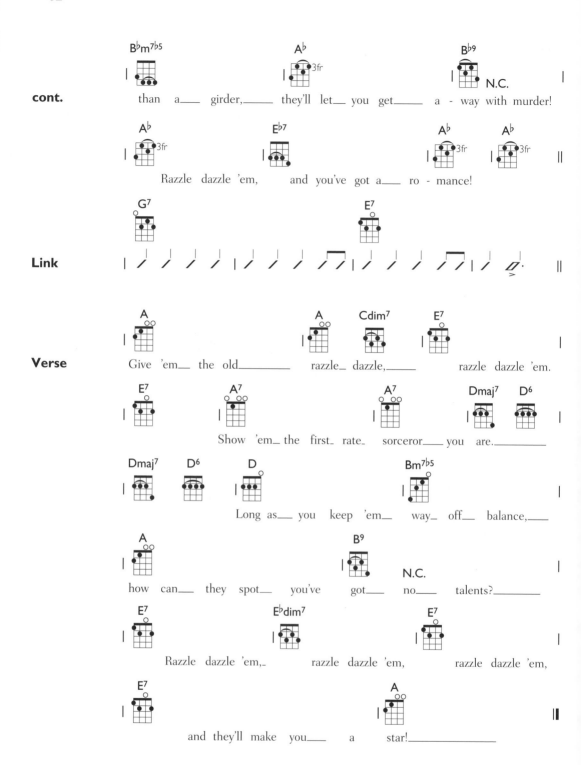

cont.

B♭m7♭5 · · A♭ 3fr · · B♭9 · · N.C. · ·

than a— girder,— they'll let— you get— a - way with murder!

A♭ 3fr · · E♭7 · · A♭ 3fr · · A♭ 3fr ·

Razzle dazzle 'em, and you've got a— ro - mance!

Link

G7 · · E7 · ·

| ╱ ╱ ╱ ╱ ╱ | ╱ ╱ ╱ ╱ ╱ | ╱ ╱ ╱ ╱ ╱ | ╱ ♩. |

Verse

A · · A · · Cdim7 · · E7 · ·

Give 'em— the old_____ razzle— dazzle,_____ razzle dazzle 'em.

E7 · · A7 · · A7 · · Dmaj7 · · D6 · ·

Show 'em— the first— rate— sorceror—— you are._____

Dmaj7 · · D6 · · D · · Bm7♭5 · ·

Long as— you keep 'em— way— off— balance,____

A · · B9 · · N.C. · ·

how can— they spot— you've got— no— talents?_____

E7 · · E♭dim7 · · E7 · ·

Razzle dazzle 'em,— razzle dazzle 'em, razzle dazzle 'em,

E7 · · A · ·

and they'll make you— a star!_____

Secret Love

Words by Paul Francis Webster
Music by Sammy Fain

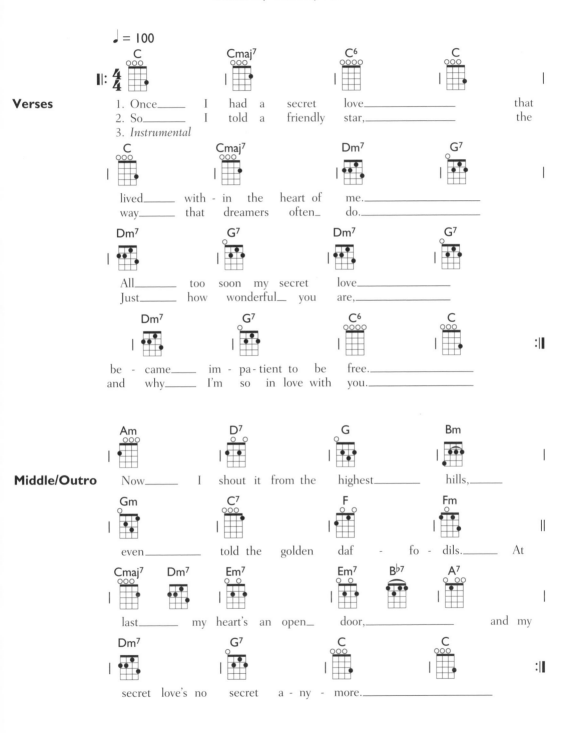

Sister Act

Words and Music by Alan Menken and Glenn Slater

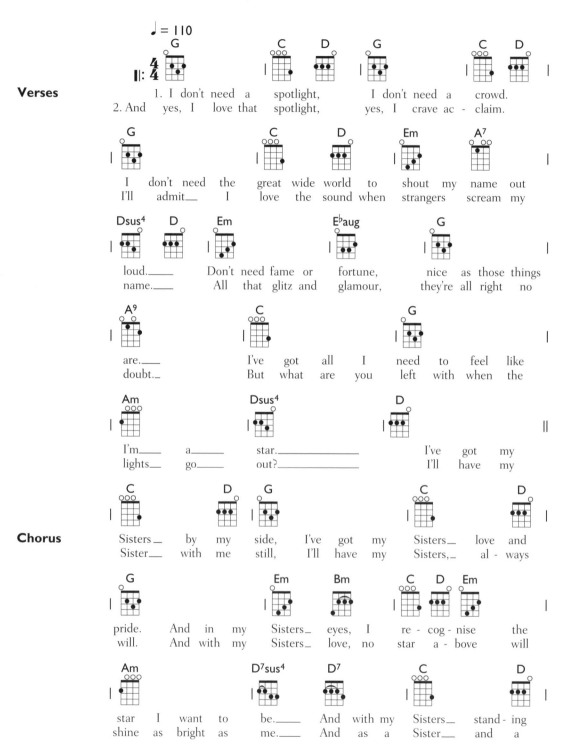

Verses

Chorus

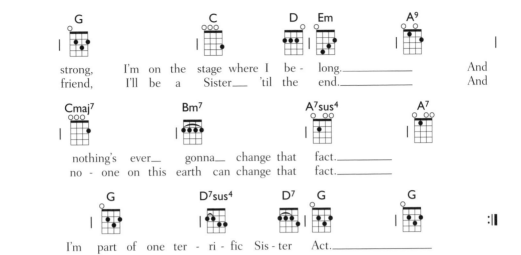

cont.

| G | C | D | Em | A⁹ |

strong,   I'm   on   the   stage   where   I   be - long._____   And
friend,   I'll   be   a   Sister___   'til   the   end._____   And

| Cmaj⁷ | Bm⁷ | A⁷sus⁴ | A⁷ |

nothing's   ever___   gonna___   change   that   fact._____
no - one   on   this   earth   can   change   that   fact._____

| G | D⁷sus⁴ | D⁷ | G | G |

I'm   part   of   one   ter - ri - fic   Sis - ter   Act._____

Stranger In Paradise

Words and Music by George Chet Forrest and Bob Wright

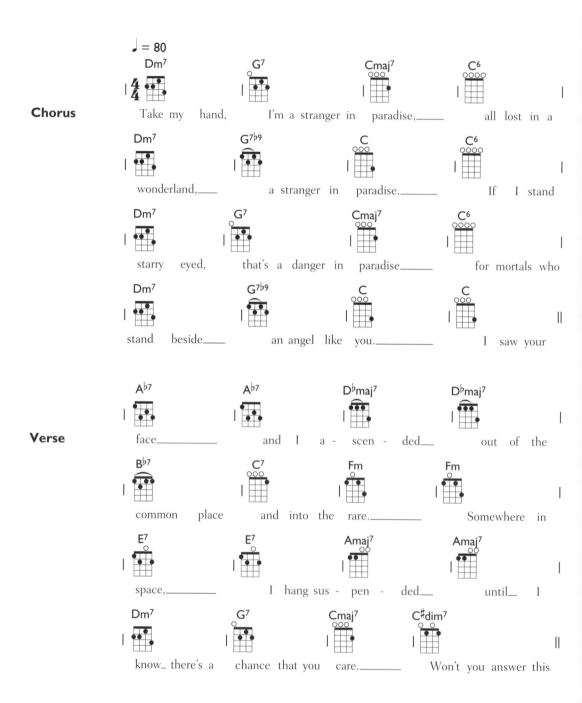

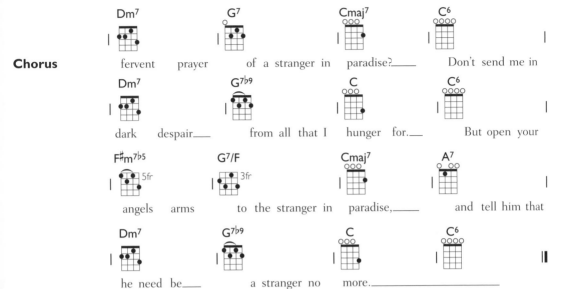

Chorus

Dm⁷	G⁷	Cmaj⁷	C⁶
fervent prayer	of a stranger in	paradise?___	Don't send me in

Dm⁷	G⁷♭⁹	C	C⁶
dark despair___	from all that I	hunger for.___	But open your

F♯m⁷♭⁵	G⁷/F	Cmaj⁷	A⁷
angels arms	to the stranger in	paradise,___	and tell him that

Dm⁷	G⁷♭⁹	C	C⁶
he need be___	a stranger no	more._____	

Summertime

Music and Lyrics by George Gershwin, Du Bose Heyward
and Dorothy Heyward and Ira Gershwin

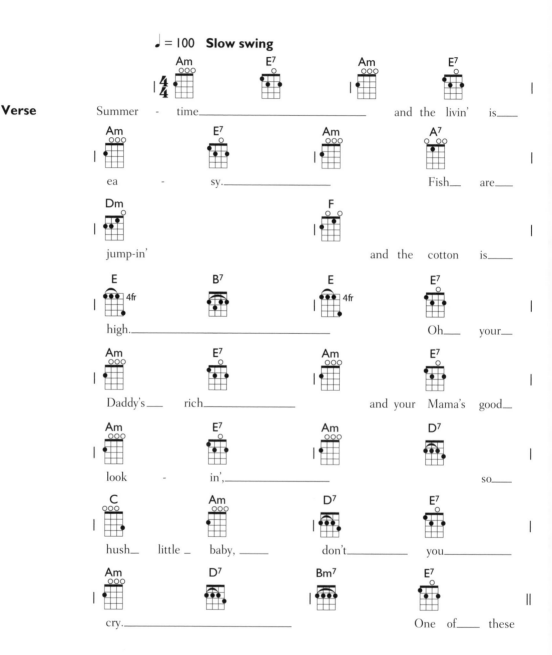

cont.

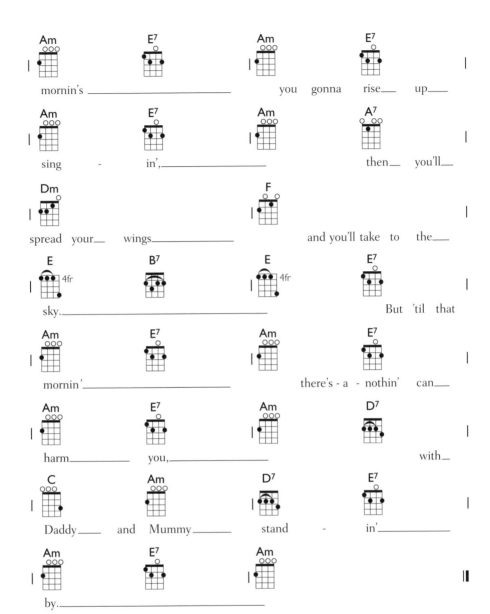

Am	E⁷	Am	E⁷
mornin's _____		you gonna	rise___ up___

Am	E⁷	Am	A⁷
sing -	in',_____		then___ you'll___

Dm	F
spread your___ wings_____	and you'll take to the___

E (4fr)	B⁷	E (4fr)	E⁷
sky._____			But 'til that

Am	E⁷	Am	E⁷
mornin'_____		there's - a - nothin'	can___

Am	E⁷	Am	D⁷
harm_____ you,_____			with_

C	Am	D⁷	E⁷
Daddy____ and Mummy_____		stand -	in'_____

Am	E⁷	Am
by._____		

Tomorrow

Lyric by Martin Charnin
Music by Charles Strouse

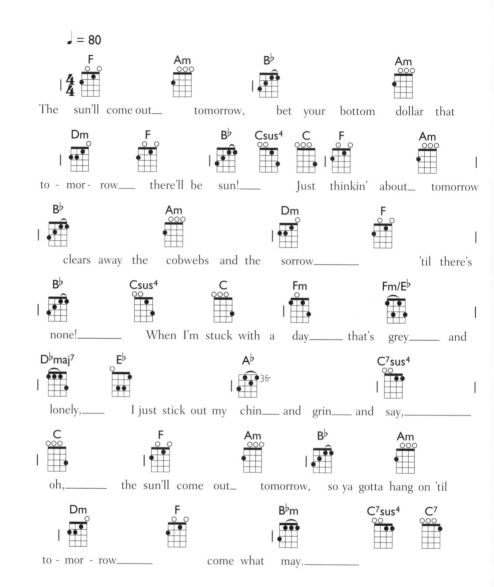

Verse

♩ = 80

F — The sun'll come out__ tomorrow,

Am — bet your bottom

Bb — dollar that

Am

Dm — to-mor-row__

F — there'll be

Bb Csus4 C — sun!__ Just

F — thinkin' about__

Am — tomorrow

Bb — clears away the

Am — cobwebs and the

Dm — sorrow_____

F — 'til there's

Bb — none!_____

Csus4 — When I'm stuck with a

C — day_____ that's

Fm — grey_____ and

Fm/Eb

Dbmaj7 — lonely,____

Eb — I just stick out my

Ab 3fr — chin__ and grin__ and

C7sus4 — say,_____

C — oh,_____

F — the sun'll come out__

Am — tomorrow,

Bb — so ya gotta hang on 'til

Am

Dm — to-mor-row_____

F — come what

Bbm — may._____

C7sus4 C7

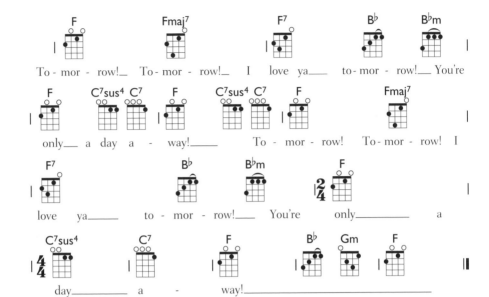

Chorus

To - mor - row!_ To - mor - row!_ I love ya___ to - mor - row!__ You're

only__ a day a - way!____ To - mor - row! To - mor - row! I

love ya____ to - mor - row!___ You're only_____ a

day_____ a - way!_____

Too Darn Hot

Words and Music by Cole Porter

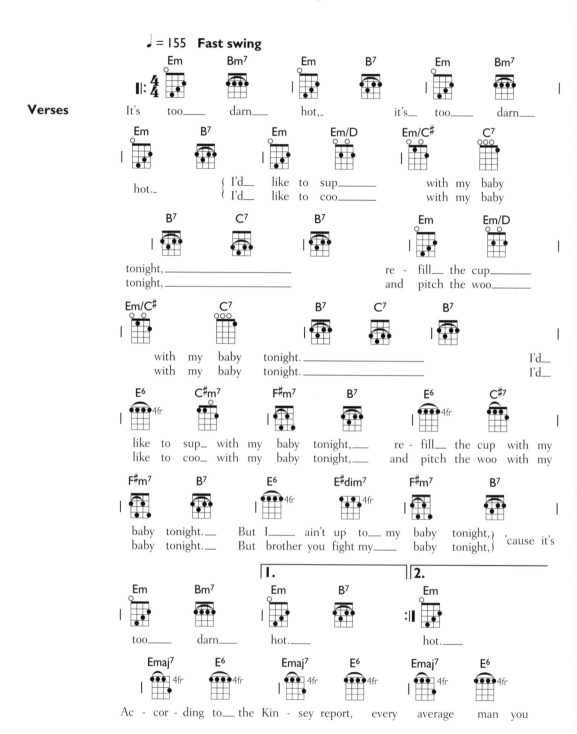

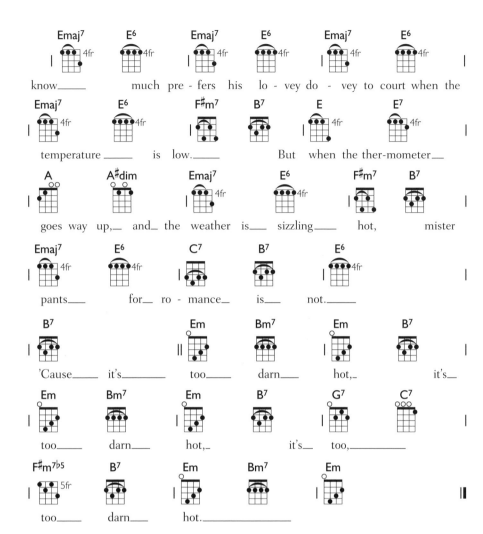

cont.

Emaj⁷ | E⁶ | Emaj⁷ | E⁶ | Emaj⁷ | E⁶

know_____ much pre - fers his lo - vey do - vey to court when the

Emaj⁷ | E⁶ | F#m⁷ | B⁷ | E | E⁷

temperature _____ is low._____ But when the ther-mometer___

A | A#dim | Emaj⁷ | E⁶ | F#m⁷ | B⁷

goes way up,_ and_ the weather is__ sizzling_____ hot, mister

Emaj⁷ | E⁶ | C⁷ | B⁷ | E⁶

pants___ for_ ro - mance_ is__ not._____

B⁷ | Em | Bm⁷ | Em | B⁷

'Cause_____ it's_____ too_____ darn_____ hot,_ it's__

Em | Bm⁷ | Em | B⁷ | G⁷ | C⁷

too_____ darn_____ hot,_ it's__ too,_____

F#m⁷♭5 | B⁷ | Em | Bm⁷ | Em

too_____ darn___ hot._____

What I Did For Love

Words by Edward Kleban
Music by Marvin Hamlisch

♩ = 85

G   E⁷sus⁴   E⁷

Verses

1. Kiss today good - bye,_____ the sweetness_ and the
2. Look, my eyes are dry,_____ the gift was ours to

Am   Cm⁶   G   D   A⁷

sorrow._____ Wish me luck, the same_ to_____ you,_____
borrow._____ It's as if we al - ways_ knew,_____

A⁷   Cm   Cm⁶

but I can't re - gret what I did for_ love,____ what I did for_
and I won't for - get what I did for_ love,____ what I did for_

1.   **2.**

D⁷   D⁷   B⁷sus⁴   B⁷

love._____
love._____

Em   Cmaj⁷ B⁷sus⁴ B⁷ Em   C♯m⁷♭⁵ F♯⁷

Bridge

Gone,_____ love is never gone,_____ as we travel

Bm   E⁷sus⁴ E⁷♭⁹   Am⁷♭⁵   D⁷

on,_____ love's what we'll re - member._____

G   E⁷sus⁴ E⁷   Am

Verse

Kiss today good - bye,_____ and point me t'ward to - morrow._____

Cm⁶   G   D   Em   A⁷

We did what we had____ to_____ do,_____

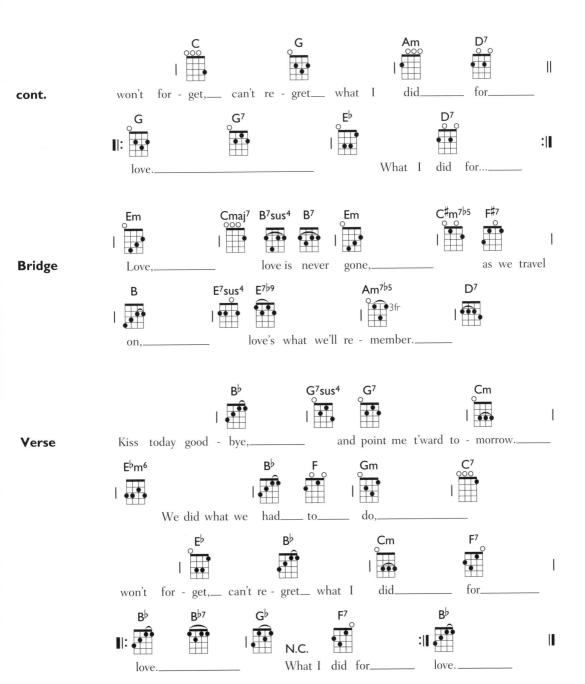

cont. won't for - get,___ can't re - gret___ what I did_____ for_____

love._____ What I did for..._____

Bridge Love,_____ love is never gone,_____ as we travel

on,_____ love's what we'll re - member._____

Verse Kiss today good - bye,_____ and point me t'ward to - morrow._____

We did what we had___ to_____ do,_____

won't for - get,___ can't re - gret___ what I did_____ for_____

love._____ What I did for_____ love._____

Wouldn't It Be Loverly?

Words by Alan Jay Lerner
Music by Frederick Loewe

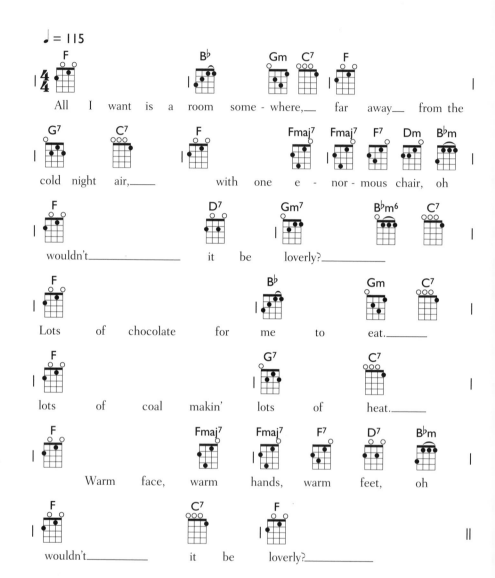

Verse

♩ = 115

All I want is a room some - where,___ far away___ from the cold night air,_____ with one e - nor - mous chair, oh wouldn't_____ it be loverly?_____ Lots of chocolate for me to eat._____ lots of coal makin' lots of heat._____ Warm face, warm hands, warm feet, oh wouldn't_____ it be loverly?_____

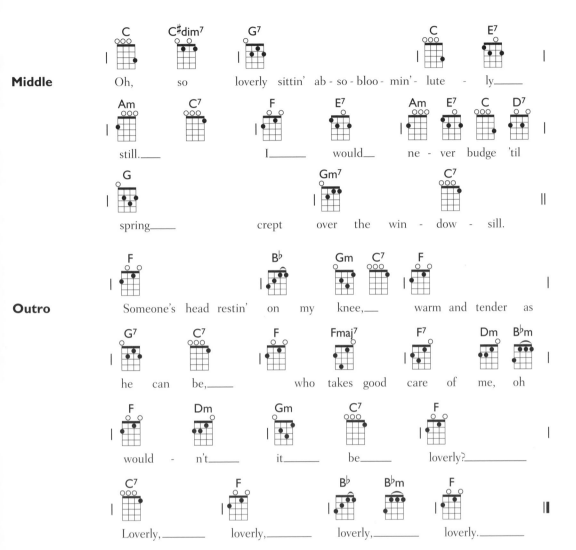

Middle

C   C#dim⁷   G⁷   C   E⁷

Oh,   so   loverly sittin' ab - so - bloo - min' - lute - ly____

Am   C⁷   F   E⁷   Am   E⁷   C   D⁷

still.____   I____   would__   ne - ver budge 'til

G   Gm⁷   C⁷

spring____   crept   over   the   win - dow - sill.

Outro

F   B♭   Gm   C⁷   F

Someone's head restin'   on   my   knee,____   warm and tender as

G⁷   C⁷   F   Fmaj⁷   F⁷   Dm   B♭m

he   can   be,____   who   takes good   care   of   me,   oh

F   Dm   Gm   C⁷   F

would - n't____   it____   be____   loverly?____

C⁷   F   B♭   B♭m   F

Loverly,____   loverly,____   loverly,____   loverly.____

Supercalifragilisticexpialidocious

Words and Music by Richard M. Sherman and Robert B. Sherman

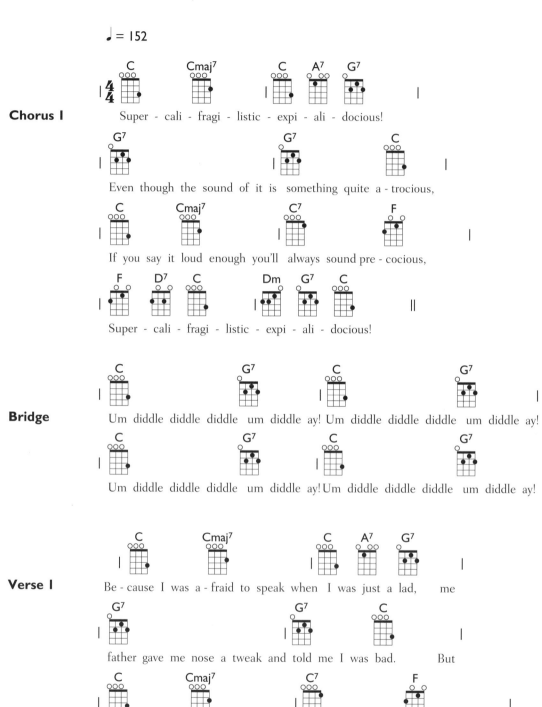

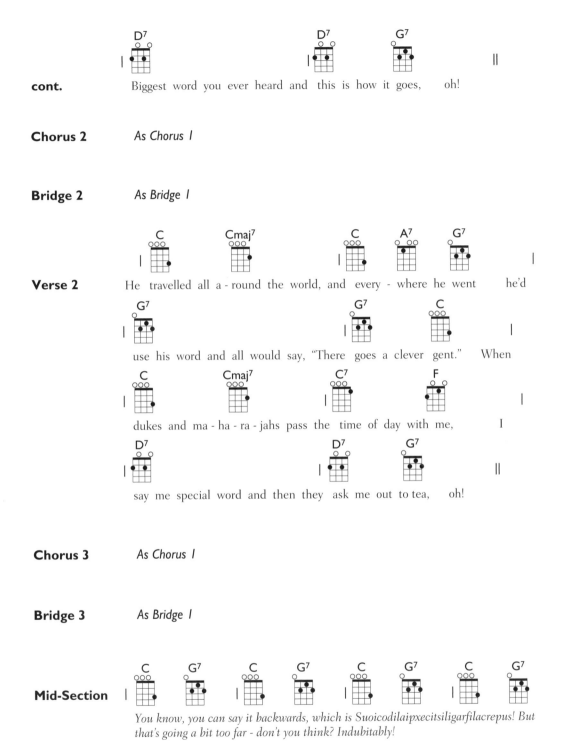

cont.   Biggest word you ever heard and this is how it goes,   oh!

Chorus 2   *As Chorus 1*

Bridge 2   *As Bridge 1*

Verse 2   He travelled all a - round the world, and every - where he went   he'd

use his word and all would say, "There goes a clever gent."   When

dukes and ma - ha - ra - jahs pass the time of day with me,   I

say me special word and then they ask me out to tea,   oh!

Chorus 3   *As Chorus 1*

Bridge 3   *As Bridge 1*

Mid-Section   *You know, you can say it backwards, which is Suoicodilaipxecitsiligarfilacrepus! But that's going a bit too far - don't you think? Indubitably!*

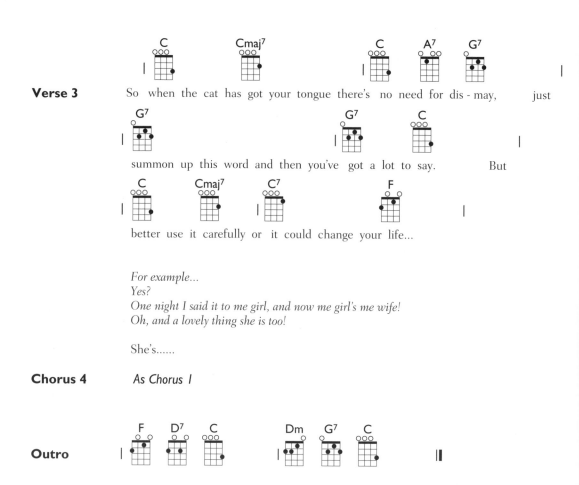

Verse 3   So when the cat has got your tongue there's no need for dis - may,   just

summon up this word and then you've got a lot to say.   But

better use it carefully or it could change your life...

For example...
Yes?
One night I said it to me girl, and now me girl's me wife!
Oh, and a lovely thing she is too!

She's......

Chorus 4   *As Chorus 1*

Outro